COACHING AND MOTIVATION:

A Practical Guide to Maximum Athletic Performance

WILLIAM E. WARREN

COACHING AND MOTIVATION:

A Practical Guide to Maximum Athletic Performance

PRENTICE-HALL, INC.
ENGLEWOOD CLIFFS, N.J.

Prentice-Hall International, Inc., *London*
Prentice-Hall of Australia, Pty. Ltd., *Sydney*
Prentice-Hall of Canada, Ltd., *Toronto*
Prentice-Hall of India Private Ltd., *New Delhi*
Prentice-Hall of Japan, Inc., *Tokyo*
Prentice-Hall of Southeast Asia Pte. Ltd., *Singapore*
Whitehall Books, Ltd., *Wellington, New Zealand*

© 1983 *by*

Prentice-Hall, Inc.
Englewood Cliffs, New Jersey

10 9 8 7 6 5 4 3 2

Library of Congress Cataloging in Publication Data

Warren, William E.,
   Coaching and motivation.

   Bibliography: p.
   Includes index.
   1. Coaching (Athletics) 2. Motivation (Psychology)
I. Title.
GV711.G34 1983   796'.07'7   83-9671
ISBN 0-13-138990-4
ISBN 0-13-140203-X PBK

Printed in the United States of America

FOREWORD

The longer I'm associated with coaching, the more strongly I'm convinced that coaching *is* motivation. Another way of saying it is, coaching is *teaching*, and I don't think you can teach effectively for any length of time unless you can motivate your players to want to learn.

What we're after, of course, are self-disciplined, *self-motivated* athletes. But these youngsters are as scarce as quick, talented seven-footers in basketball or 250-pounders who bench-press 500 lbs. and run the 40 in 4.6 in football. The difference, as Bobby Knight has pointed out, is that you can't teach them to be seven feet tall (or lightning fast). But you *can* teach them to become self-disciplined. And in most cases you can go a long way toward teaching them to be self-motivated.

Coaching And Motivation tells you how to do it.

Coach Warren is a high school coach, but his book is equally valid for PeeWee Leagues, junior high, college or professional athletics. As he points out in Chapter 1, motivation consists of finding ways to get people to do things they might not want to do on their own. It doesn't matter whether you're coaching men or women, or sports as diverse as football, field hockey, cross-country or swimming; you still have to know how to motivate your players to give their best efforts in competition.

In developing a motivational philosophy, I think there are probably two factors a coach needs to keep in mind. First, he should be open-minded in terms of willingness to consider new techniques, since not everyone responds to the same stimuli, and even the best techniques can grow stale through overuse. Second, he should have the determination to continue to try to "reach" boys and girls who do not respond to his initial efforts.

Many different approaches to motivation are described and discussed in *Coaching And Motivation*, for the simple reason that the subject requires broad treatment. There is no single, simple way of motivating everyone, just as there is no single formula for winning. Many of my own ideas on motivation are included in the present volume but I am not so vain as to suggest that they will work for everyone. You have to do what you do best, and in the best way you can.

Jerry Tarkanian

INTRODUCTION

This is the eighth book I've written or co-authored. It is by far the most ambitious project I've undertaken to date—and it has been the most difficult to write, for the simple reason that motivation in team sports involves the human personality's interacting with other humans, other personalities. And because motivation involves *personalities* and *relationships* rather than Xs and Os on chalkboards, it is open-ended to the extent that the theories upon which motivation is based are always open to question. They are *theories*, not commandments etched in stone.

That's the bad news. The *good* news is that it doesn't really matter whether you prefer Maslow's theory of motivation based on a hierarchy of needs, or Thorndike's reinforcement theory of motivation, or any of the other motivational theories. They are not mutually exclusive. Just as 2,000 years ago it was said "All roads lead to Rome," so it is that any or all of the most widely held theories of how people are motivated may be valid for your own situation, depending upon your philosophy and your understanding of how you best relate to your players.

In his book *The Elements Of Style*, the late William Strunk stated that every writer should always keep three objectives in mind when he is writing: clarity, clarity, clarity. Thus, in writing this book, I have chosen to use a practical, informal style rather than run the risk of tying you, the reader, in verbal knots through the use of a more technical approach to the subject of motivation.

This does not mean that the information herein contained is any less valid than if I flogged you with technical terms and the somewhat lofty and nebulous language of the social sciences. What it *does* mean is that:

(a) You will not need a collegiate dictionary, *Roget's Thesaurus*, and a copy of your old Ed Psy 201 book close at hand to understand, enjoy and learn from this book; and

(b) Because you understand the subject matter, you will be able to properly evaluate the ideas and techniques presented.

In this book, I've taken the three elements of team sports—the coach, the players, and the sport—and analyzed ways that coaches can resolve conflicts or problems that arise among or within these elements.[1] In the process, I have described my own views concerning the relationships between coach, players and sport that are most conducive to successfully motivating athletes. But I also have drawn upon the collective wisdom of many other persons, in and out of coaching, not merely to support my own views but also to provide the broadest possible view of why athletes think and act as they do, why motivation is necessary, and what coaches have done (and can do) to bridge the gap that separates us from our players.

Specifically, I've attempted to provide a broad spectrum of viewpoints and answers regarding the following questions, problems and issues:

*What's so difficult about motivation? Aren't *all* athletes motivated?

*Which is more important, short-term (day-to-day) motivation or a long-range motivational program?

*Is it possible to identify the forces at work in motivating athletes?

*Are there different styles of motivation a coach can use?

*Can you suggest guidelines for coaches to consider in dealing with and motivating young people? (Twenty-four guidelines are presented which, when taken together, form the basis for an organized and consistent approach to motivation.)

*I've seen teams whose players fairly *oozed* confidence, dedication and pride. Is it possible to build that kind of attitude in your teams, or do you have to wait until you get that special kind of player?

*Why is the first year of coaching in a new situation so difficult? How do you go about surviving that first year?

*How do you build a successful program in terms of motivation?

*How effective are rewards and incentives as motivators?

*How effective is punishment likely to be as a teaching method/motivational device? Should I discipline my players?

---

[1]Obviously, if no conflicts or problems exist, external motivation such as that provided by the coach is unnecessary.

*Can players be taught to handle pressure situations effectively?

* What can the coach do to make daily practices seem less routine and boring?

* How should you handle the problem of players who don't like to practice?

*What should you say in your pre-game, halftime and post-game talks?

* How do you go about getting your players "up" for easy opponents?

*Do gimmicks and stunts really work? How do you go about setting them up?

* How can you build positive team attitudes and relationships among your players?

*Why aren't all of my players self-motivated? Is there anything I should know about dealing with self-motivated athletes?

* How far should a coach go in trying to work with problem athletes? Where do you draw the line between individual and team needs when conflicts arise between the two? Can habitual rules-breakers be saved?

*Should you try to treat your superstar athlete the same as everyone else? What problems are you likely to have with this kind of player?

*Are there special problems associated with coaching women? Are women harder to motivate than men? What motivational approaches are likely to work best with women?

*Is it necessary to motivate your reserves and bench-warmers as well as your regulars? How do you motivate players who don't get to play much?

*Do assistant coaches require external motivation? What can the head coach do to motivate his/her assistants?

*Do the motivational challenges facing the coach change in the course of the season? What can the coach do to maintain a high degree of player motivation when facing the prospect of a losing season?

Although most of us face a multitude of coaching-related tasks in our work (e.g., scheduling, budgeting, maintaining equipment and facilities, filling out eligibility reports, etc.), the coaching task itself can be reduced to two areas, *teaching* and *motivation*. We teach youngsters the skills, patterns and strategies necessary to play a given sport, and then we motivate them to give their best efforts in playing the game.

Obviously, the better teacher a coach is, the more his/her players will learn in terms of skills, patterns and strategy—assuming, of course, that the coach possesses a basic understanding of the skills, patterns and strategy associated with his sport. What is *not* so obvious or well understood by coaches is the fact that motivation involves far more than pep rallies, slogans on locker room walls, and inspirational pre-game or halftime talks to the players. Those are merely the tip of the iceberg, the visible 15 percent that is most often associated with motivation. It is the other 85 percent of motivation—the unseen but vitally important formation of positive attitudes and relationships among players and coaches—with which this book is primarily concerned.

Perhaps the best place to start is to analyze your own concept of motivation. In this regard, it should be helpful for me to state that I have never known a successful coach in any sport, or on any level of play, who does not consider motivation to be an ongoing process, one which requires careful planning and constant attention. Pre-game and halftime talks are undeniably important—but they are not where motivation begins or ends, any more than they are the most desirable setting for teaching new skills, patterns or strategies.

When I was a youngster trying out for my school's basketball team for the first time, I remember the coach addressing us as we waited in the bleachers for tryouts to begin. "Fellas," he said, "this round thing in my hands is a basketball . . ."

Chapter 1, "An Introduction To Motivation," begins at precisely the same point where motivation is concerned, by defining the terms and the scope of the problem.

Now, let's go out there and win one for the Gipper!

                                                                    William E. Warren

CONTENTS

PART ONE—AN INTRODUCTION TO MOTIVATION

8. **Motivation and the Program** (*continued*)

PART THREE—MOTIVATIONAL TECHNIQUES

PART FOUR—SITUATIONAL MOTIVATION

14. Forging Positive Attitudes and Relationships *(continued)*

15. Handling the Self-Motivated Athlete 143

16. Motivating the "Problem" Athlete........................... 147

17. Handling the "Superstar" Athlete 157

18. Motivating Girls and Women 165

For

Louise, George and Wendi Warren

and for
four great motivators:

Coach Jerry Tarkanian, Head Basketball Coach
at the University of Nevada at Las Vegas;

Coach Larry Chapman, Head Basketball Coach
at Auburn University at Montgomery;

The late Coach Paul "Bear" Bryant; and

The late Coach Vince Lombardi

PART ONE

AN INTRODUCTION TO MOTIVATION

CHAPTER 1

A New Definition of Motivation

Motivation. It's the kind of word all of us understand, as long as we don't have to define it: "Sure, I know what motivation is . . . it's—it's, uh, well, uh—it's what you've done a good job of when your team wins by thirty points when you were supposed to lose by that amount."

But all of us know, too, that there's much, much more to motivation than that.

Dictionary definitions generally fall short of telling us any more about motivation. A random survey of popular dictionaries reveals the following definitions: "the act or an instance of being motivated"; "the state or condition of being motivated;" and "that which motivates; inducement; incentive." Not much to go on there, though. These definitions approach the problem obliquely, if at all. True, motivation is the creation or presence of motives, incentives or inducements. The Great Pyramids at Gizeh are blocks of stone, too. But describing the Pyramids as "blocks of stone" hardly does justice to the unique features which rank them among the Seven Wonders of the World.

No, what we need at this point is a new definition of motivation that fits the unique requirements of athletic competition. Let us, therefore, begin by throwing out the dictionary definitions, and formulate new definitions for motivation in terms of coaching and playing in sports:

> To coaches, motivation means *finding ways to get players to do things they might not want to do on their own.*
> To players, motivation means *having reasons for acting or failing to act.*

The disparity between these two viewpoints, including potential conflicts of interests between coaches and players, is what this book—and, indeed, much of coaching—is all about.

PRELIMINARY CONSIDERATIONS

The aspect of motivation which concerns coaches most greatly is that of preparing players to give optimal performances in games. That no coach has ever been—or ever will be—completely successful in this regard is obvious. That the problem is of paramount importance to every coach is equally apparent. Perhaps we may never be able to create a final, definitive statement of what motivation really is. We can, however, list and investigate the elements of player preparation and performance which require motivation, and in so doing we can come to a fuller understanding of how optimal performances arise.

Motivation for What?

It's natural for people to look for shortcuts to success. Even though we may know in our hearts that there are no shortcuts or easy paths to athletic excellence, most of us would prefer to follow the path of least resistance to success. Players who by their nature are willing to forgo "easy" solutions to problems and give total effort in their athletic performances are known as *self-activated*, or *self-motivated*, athletes. They are a rare breed, and growing scarcer in number with each passing year.

As technological advances continue to improve the quality of life in our modern world, coaches are, with increasing frequency, finding it necessary to study their motivational techniques to discover new ways to persuade youngsters to participate in athletics, or to improve the quality of their athletic performances. Why, after all, should young people elect to undergo the rigors of athletic training when, with less effort, they could be watching television, experimenting with drugs, wheeling around the neighborhood with their girlfriends or boyfriends, or otherwise preoccupying themselves with matters non-athletic?

Motivation Toward Winning

Traditionally, athletes have been motivated by the desire to win. Being *Number One*. That's what the "American Dream" is all about. Even the official Little League baseball rule book has pointed out that the primary purpose of baseball is to outscore the opponents.

The American Dream grew tarnished over the decades of the '60s and '70s, as many observers inside and outside of sports decried the "win at all costs" philosophy that they saw pervading our nation's politics as well as its sport philosophy. The result was a backlash against participation in team sports in general, in favor of physical activities such as jogging, hang gliding, sky diving, surfing, body building, dance, skating, and other noncompetitive activities. Now, it is admirable for anyone to participate in sport of any sort, whether competitive or otherwise, particularly in our age of spectatorism. But those who deny all values of competitive sports simply because there happens to be a loser every time someone wins are as misguided as those who consider winning to be the *only* acceptable outcome of athletic competition. Winning *is* important—surely no one enters competition for the expressed purpose of losing!—but there is such a thing as *victory in defeat*, too.

In my second year of coaching at Toombs Central High School, my basketball team won 25 games and lost only 2—but it was one of the most miserable years I've ever spent in coaching. The players didn't like each other, and they didn't like me. They couldn't wait to get out of the dressing room after games so they could go their own separate ways. Consequently, there was relatively little sense of joy or accomplishment associated with our victories. Then, the team leaders graduated, and although our record dropped to 14-9 the following year, the returning players and I enjoyed the season immensely. We weren't at all a highly skilled team, but we were a *team* in the very best sense of the word, in victory and in defeat.

I decided then and there that I'd rather lose occasionally with players who are willing to run into walls for the team, than to win every game with more talented youngsters who don't care about each other.

For me, at least, victory isn't what shows up on the scoreboard at the end of games; it's what shows up on a youngster's *heart*, as evidenced by the manner in which he/she plays the game. I'll take the ones who *care*, the ones who display a genuine sense of dedication and responsibility to me and their teammates, every time, regardless of their skills. If they care, I can *teach* them the skills they'll need in competition. I can motivate them. And when we lose—well, I've found that it's not so hard to accept defeat when your team has given everything it has toward winning. It's never fun to lose—and I probably want to win as much as any coach alive—but I don't have trouble getting to sleep at night after losses in which my players gave their best efforts to play the game the way I wanted it played.

Motivation Toward Individual Excellence

While all athletes prefer winning to losing, not all athletes are willing to give the kind of physical and mental effort necessary to win games. They *should* be willing, but the gulf between what *should be* and what *is* sometimes is enormous.

Our world is becoming one in which apathy and satisfaction with mediocrity are the rule rather than the exception. Sports offers participants the opportunity to pursue excellence and overcome adversity, and in the process to extend themselves to the limits of their ability.

Coaches are naturally concerned about winning; in many cases, their jobs depend on it. Still, a coach is making a grave mistake if he gets so caught up in wanting to win that he overlooks other considerations that motivate players toward excellence. Players should be encouraged constantly toward their limits. While not every athlete is equally committed to winning, every athlete should be committed to the quest for personal excellence.

Motivation Toward Team Goals

It is virtually impossible to be, or to become, an outstanding athlete in team sports without learning to sacrifice somewhere along the way. First, a beginning athlete sacrifices time that could be spent doing other things to learn the skills associated with his/her sport. Then, having acquired those skills, the athlete learns that one's role as a team member usually requires further sacrifices, such as abiding by team rules, getting along with the coach and one's teammates, and learning to function as part of a team rather than as an individual. Team membership involves discipline, whether external or self-imposed, and this in turn requires a willingness to sacrifice personal goals for team goals when necessary.

Being part of a team united in the pursuit of common goals can be an uplifting experience. Where such a state exists, with players performing in an atmosphere of mutual commitment and respect, the coach will have little problem motivating players. When the players are motivated by a continuing sense of obligation to their team and teammates, the coach's short-term motivational tactics are, in all likelihood, going to pay off in huge dividends.

The problem lies in fostering that kind of attitude among your players. It's all part—the most important part—of building a successful program in your sport.

Other Motivators

It would be possible, with only minimal effort, to write volumes on the various forces at play in motivating people toward participation in sports, or toward high levels of athletic achievement within given sports. Beyond this, many of the values are virtually indescribable in terms understandable to nonparticipants.

Still, at least five motivational factors beyond those already mentioned deserve attention. First, *the development of a favorable self-concept* is important in the pursuit of team goals.

On an individual basis, a positive self-image entails pride in previous accomplishments and confidence in one's ability to success-fully perform present or future tasks. Young players, in particular, who have not participated in athletics long enough to have acquired a sense of pride in past athletic accomplishments must be handled carefully lest they grow either cocky and overconfident, or have their confidence destroyed by early failures.

A fine line exists between pride and cockiness, and between confidence and overconfidence. The wise coach will constantly be on the lookout for signs that his/her players are becoming overconfident to the point of complacence. Motivating complacent players is probably the most difficult motivational task a coach can face. Thus, since an ounce of prevention is worth a pound of cure, the coach should constantly remind his/her players of the effort winning requires.

In the same way that time and the healing process tend to blur our remembrance of pain, time also sometimes blurs an athlete's perception and memory of the hard work he or she had to put forth to become a winner. In such cases, the athlete, newly accustomed to winning, may expect to win, not by virtue of hard work and mental and physical discipline, but simply because he/she is suited up for the game. Any of several causative factors may be at work here: first, most athletes, being human, prefer, if left to their own devices, to follow the line of least resistance to success. Relatively few athletes have the self-discipline to work to maximum when they think that less than a maximum effort will suffice.

Second, many youngsters get caught up in "macho" images of how the game—any game—should be played, and working hard may not fit into their idea of the way the superior athlete (or team) operates. This concept does not arise overnight, of course; it grows within the players when they begin to forget how hard they worked in the past to become skilled athletes and winners.

Third, the athlete may subconsciously want to avoid the new-found pressures that winning brings. The habitually losing team normally faces little pressure to win, which tends to reduce that team's effectiveness in pressure situations. When that team begins to win, and thus to change its image as a loser, however, players find that winning teams always face a measure of pressure to keep on winning. And while coaches often talk to players about "playing out of their comfort zones," they—the coaches—sometimes overlook the fact that this "comfort zone" is as much mental as physical. Memories of earlier defeats can inspire players to great heights of performance, but can also lead them to slack off in pressure situations, particularly when defeat is imminent, so they can justify the defeat in their own minds on the grounds that they just weren't trying. (They're not going to tell the coach this, of course, but they can use it to justify the loss to themselves and their friends.)

Vince Lombardi held that, as difficult as winning a championship is, it is not the ultimate proof of a team's success. Lombardi contended that the true champion is the team or individual that can defend its championship the following season.

While most of us have not reached the pinnacles of success in our coaching where one-time championships can be dismissed so lightly, there is much in what Coach Lombardi said in this regard. In particular, it is a warning to players and coaches alike that, as victories mount up, the greatest obstacle to success facing a team is likely to be its own overconfidence or complacence. Or, in the words of cartoonist Walt Kelly's *Pogo*, "We have met the enemy, and he is *us*."

A second factor in the motivation of athletes is *the challenge of competition, or the opportunity to prove oneself in head-to-head competition against others.* And where teams have lost previously to an opponent, they are often motivated by a desire to restore their pride and avenge their earlier loss.

Fear is a third factor that motivates players. There are, of course, many kinds of fear—fear of losing, fear of failing to do one's best, fear of letting down one's teammates, friends, parents, schoolmates, etc., fear of the coach—and all are powerful motivators, although the latter—fear of the coach—is likely to be effective only when a team is winning regularly.[1]

Fourth, *athletics provides an outlet for aggression and pent-up energies, and provides participants with a focal point for their energies* Coaches are always on the lookout for energetic, aggressive players. Whereas aggressive players can always be taught to recognize situations that may require a passive approach (e.g., pitching around a dangerous hitter when protecting a slim lead in the late innings of a baseball game, as opposed to challenging the hitter by throwing strikes), the converse is seldom true. Passive players generally find it very difficult to play aggressively with any degree of success, even in situations in which the need for aggressive play is clearly indicated.

Fifth, *competitive sports permit players (and teams) to exert dominance over opponents.* Coach Sam Roberts (1971, p. 25) contended that the two drives that motivate runners as athletes are the desires for recognition and a sense of power over others. The vast majority of athletes who cease to run competitively, Roberts contended, do so because they lose their motivation rather than their running skills.

How important is motivation? Football Coach George Allen

---

[1]When a team is losing consistently, fear of the coach creates a highly negative atmosphere, Tiedemann (1976, p. 14) explains, and increases the likelihood of resentment or rebellion among players on the team.

(1973, p. 79) has said that, even on the professional level, a coach is mistaken if he thinks he doesn't have to movivate his players. Allen believes that everyone has to be motivated to do his job to the best of his ability—from the players to the assistant coaches to the groundskeepers and equipment managers to the secretaries in the front office.

Personally, I rate the motivational task as equal to that of preparing and studying scouting reports, game films and game plans.

Game plans, for example, are always based on assumptions of maximum effort by the team. Still, the best game plan or scouting report ever devised isn't worth the paper it's written on if the players are not motivated to carry it out properly.

According to Dr. Russ Tiedemann (1976, p. 13), somewhere between 50 percent and 90 percent of the coaching task involves motivation. I think 70 percent to 90 percent is a more accurate figure.

CHAPTER 2

Problems of Motivation

THE MISUNDERSTOOD ROLE OF MOTIVATION

Probably no phase of athletic competition is more grossly misunderstood by coaches than the area of motivation. That this should be so is somewhat surprising at first glance, too, because all coaches are interested in motivation. Coaching *is* motivation—motivation and teaching.

Still, when you think about it, it's logical that coaches sometimes misunderstand their role as motivators, or else take motivation for granted. After all, most coaches are ex-players who cared enough about their sport or activity to continue their involvement after their playing days ended. Coaches tend to be highly motivated individuals, and they sometimes have trouble understanding or dealing with players who do not share equally their enthusiasm and love for the game or activity. In many cases, coaches object to having to assume what they consider to be the demeaning role of *cheerleader* for the team, or having to take time out to try to inspire the players toward higher levels of performance when they—the coaches—could be involving themselves in what they consider to be the more important task of formulating or teaching game strategies and tactics.

Taking Motivation For Granted

A good coach is a good motivator as well as a good teacher. The coach may not be able to devise gimmicks regularly, like Grant Teaff's now-famous earthworm stunt that fired up his Baylor Bears football team to beat Texas in 1979, and he/she may not be a Knute Rockne when it comes to delivering inspirational pre-game or halftime talks—but the good coach motivates nonetheless. It is *always* a mistake to take motivation for granted.

How may motivation be taken for granted? By assuming that players are self-motivated to the extent that they do not require external motivation by the coach. By concentrating entirely on the Xs and Os, and neglecting or forgetting the personalities of the players—that is, by failing to take into account that *Os and Xs don't win or lose games; players do.*

But is a coach a cheerleader? Is it really within the province of a coach's responsibilities to his/her team to plead with, cajole, threaten, inspire, shock or otherwise motivate pre-teens, teenagers, young adults or seasoned professional athletes to do what they ought to be doing without the coach's having to resort to such tactics? A basketball coach complained:

> Sometimes when I'm talking to my players before a game, I see these blank, empty gazes staring back at me as I'm talking, and even though I know they're trying to fake it (an interest in what I'm saying), I also know their minds are on something a million light years away, and I'm hoping it's not drugs or pills or something like that. I find myself hoping it's their girlfriends they're daydreaming about, because I sure as heck don't want to have one of them freaking out on the court during the game. That'd really look good on my record!
>
> Sometimes I think I ought to just come into the dressing room for my pre-game talk wearing a clown suit, a big, red rubber nose and floppy shoes. I'd hop onto the training table and say "Hey, kids, I'm Bozo the Clown, your basketball coach, and I'm here to entertain you, and maybe convince you to hustle whenever the mood strikes

you in the game tonight! Pick a card, any card, and don't let me see it . . ." Then I'd throw in a little Gene Kelly soft shoe routine while I was telling them how important it is for them to get back on defense quickly, and maybe I'd finish off my pep talk with my "Richard Pryor In Concert" imitation that's always good for a few high fives and hand slaps, just before we go out to try to raise our record to 10–7.

Am I cynical? Sure I am, but I just don't like the idea of entrusting my job security to the whims of 16- and 17-year old kids whose interest rises and falls faster than the presidential popularity polls.

I think I'm a pretty good motivator. I try to reach the kids, but sometimes it just gets to be too much for me. I get tired of trying to get them to do the things I never had to be asked to do when I was playing.

A veteran coach with more than twenty years of coaching experience viewed the problem from a slightly different perspective:

The patterns haven't changed all that much over the years. Emphasis has shifted back and forth between offense and defense, and sometimes they (the coaches) have come up with new names and approaches to old techniques, but the game is basically the same one we played when I was coming along.

What has changed most drastically has been the players' attitudes toward the game. Oh, they're highly skilled—we've never had as many outstanding athletes in every sport as we have now—but they don't get as fired up any more, and they aren't fundamentally sound. They have these tremendous natural skills, but they don't spend the time we spent learning to execute the fundamentals correctly. With the exception of George Brett, for example, I don't see kids coming along in baseball who are willing to practice the art of hitting until their hands bleed like Ted Williams did. In basketball, I see kids who can sky 40" or more in their vertical jump, but they can't play defense without hand-checking,[1] and they act like it's a violation of the rules to execute the fundamentals correctly.

What all this means for the coach is that *you have to be a motivator.* It's always been important for coaches to motivate their players, but it takes a delicate touch to teach and motivate at the same time. You have to motivate kids nowadays just to teach them the fundamentals.

---

[1] Placing one or both hands on the dribbler to control, retard or influence his movement.

SHORT-TERM VS. LONG-TERM MOTIVATION

Part of the problem coaches face in dealing with motivation arises when they confuse short-term and long-term motivational goals. Short-term motivation involves getting ready for today, for the next game; long-term motivation involves the kind of continuing commitment that is found in all kinds of successful sports programs. While both short- and long-term motivation are unquestionably vital to a team's preparation, some coaches tend to overlook long-term motivation in their haste to get players "up" for today's practice or game. True, successful programs are built a day at a time, a game at a time, but the pep talks and inspirational speeches can carry you just so far before your players begin to feel that they've heard it all before. And when or if you reach that point, you're likely to find your words bouncing off your players like bb's fired at a rhino's hide.

We'll have more to say later about long-term motivational techniques,[2] but at this juncture we'll point out that of the two—short-term and long-term motivation—the latter is infinitely more important. Long-term motivational goals include building pride, loyalty and commitment to excellence, both individually and as a team.

CHANGES WITHIN OUR SOCIETY

The decade of the '70s involved, among other things, the rise of what author Tom Wolfe has called the "Me-Now" generation; it was, in other words, a decade in which self-centeredness and the cult of the individual reigned supreme. Whereas the '60s were a time of rebellion and protest against the Establishment and symbols of recognized authority, the '70s were a quieter time when "different strokes for different folks," "doing your own thing," and "finding out who you are" became catch-phrases for a generation obsessed with the idea of gratifying itself at all costs.

Humorist James Thurber once observed that "It isn't as easy to fool little girls as it used to be." It's not easy to fool *any* young person

---

[2]See Chapter 9.

today. They all know what feels good. In too many cases, they have decided that what is important in life is whatever makes them feel good, and as a result they tend to resent the intrusion of any kind of externally imposed discipline into their lives. Practically nobody disagrees with or corrects them any more, whether at school or at home. They resent falsity and lies—yet so many of them are willing to trade reality for a drug-induced vision of the way life ought to be. Their quest is one of self-discovery (whatever that is), and they are guided by a thousand false prophets who conveniently overlook the idea that you can discover things about yourself by *giving* as well as by *taking*.

The quick high, the cheap thrill, the one-way ticket to anywhere that looks like fun: these are the hallmarks of today's society that draw many of our young people away from more productive activities and interests.

Possibly because of the kinds of problems described, many coaches have complained in recent years about how difficult coaching has become. It may seem paradoxical in light of my previous statements about the problems of today's youth, but I disagree wholeheartedly with those coaches who contend that coaching is more difficult today than ever before; in fact, I think that those coaches who are willing to meet the challenges of coaching in today's world head-on will agree that, in many respects, building winning programs is easier today than ever before—and for the very reasons described previously. Coaching is, unquestionably, different today from what it was twenty years ago—the players and society have both changed enormously in that time span—but the best coaches are still the hardest workers. That much, at least, will never change.

Values Beyond Change in Changing Times

There's an old saying that "In the kingdom of the blind, the one-eyed man is king." In coaching you can, of course, win by virtue of superior personnel, which is the easiest way to win since it involves the line of least resistance to success. Some coaches believe that this factor—personnel superiority—is the major factor in building winning teams. I don't. I think that *hard work*, *hustle* and *dedication* are the primary ingredients in building winning teams and strong programs. And since relatively few young people either fully understand the value of hard work in athletics or are willing (or, in some cases, challenged) to give a total effort to become superior athletes, the coach who conditions his/her athletes both physically and mentally to play up to 100 percent of their ability will defeat many superior opponents whose efforts never rise above 40 percent. The coach who can, through hard work, love for his/her sport and a genuine concern for young people, attract even a handful of youngsters who are willing to consider the possibility that working hard and playing hard are not detrimental to their health or well-being, will seldom, if ever, have trouble motivating players.

You can motivate dedicated players, and players who believe in you, your program and their teammates. You cannot motivate players who feel no sense of responsibility or commitment to you, your program or their teammates.

Your task, then, is obvious: to surround yourself with players who love the sport; who respect you as coach and believe that what you're trying to do for the team is best for them as well; who respect their teammates and feel a genuine need to perform well for their teammates' sake as well as their own; who are willing to put in the necessary hours to learn, and then to improve, the skills associated with their sport; and who don't consider requiring them to play hard to be a kind of punishment. You can motivate those kinds of athletes.

Providing a Favorable Setting for Motivation

"Train up a child in the way he should grow; and when he is old, he will not depart from it." These words from the book of Proverbs are as true now as they were more than 2,500 years ago when they were written. In my own case, I've had so many occasions when I've felt grateful for the players on my teams who hustle and work hard to improve themselves as athletes. But reverse the situation: should they—my players—feel grateful that I care enough about them to work as hard as I can to try to improve their skills and build a winning program? No, it was a decision I made when I started coaching, that I was going to be as good a coach as I possibly could be, and that I was not going to let other coaches or my own players outwork me.

Your players should be given the opportunity to make the same choice. What kind of players are they going to be, selfish or committed to team goals? Apathetic or dedicated? Lazy or hard-working? We, as coaches, have it in our power to greatly influence our players in this regard, first, by the example we set for them by our own efforts, and second, by our expectations for them.

Surrounding Yourself with Believers

Should you insert seniors into your starting lineup solely on the basis of their being seniors? Not if it means that the team's performance will suffer for it, or that better players will receive less playing time. Why, then, should you attempt to build your program around players who by their on-court or off-court behavior show a total lack of respect or concern for what you and the other players are trying to accomplish?

Not every player must be (or can be) as dedicated to the team concept and winning as the coach is. But in too many cases we as coaches accept as gospel truth the contentions that "Kids nowadays don't care about sports the way they used to," and that "If you work your kids too hard, they'll quit on you." Many of the kids *won't* care, of course, and they'll quit when the going gets rough. But many other young people are simply waiting for someone to guide them and care about them—and *those* are the youngsters we have to find. But if we accept as true that none of them will accept the challenge of excelling in an age of mediocrity, we're doing them a grave disservice: we're prejudging them toward the same mediocrity we want them to avoid. And we're underestimating by light-years their potential for dedication and commitment. Sure, ours is an age of individualism—but not all young people are selfish. And maybe many of those potential athletes who come to us with a "what's-in-it-for-me?" attitude have never had the opportunity to give of themselves toward a purpose beyond themselves.

Pursuing Team Goals

The spirit of willingness to sacrifice oneself to whatever extent is necessary to further team goals is currently out of vogue in many circles; still, it is potentially one of the greatest pluses to be derived from participating in team sports. Just as the coach cannot be all things to all people, the athlete cannot be all things for himself in all situations. Does an athlete lose his individuality, or become less a person, when, for example, he sacrifice-bunts to advance a teammate in baseball, or passes to an open teammate in basketball, soccer or hockey rather than taking the shot at goal himself? Of course not. He is merely substituting team goals for those that serve only to advance or promote his own performance.

And sure, ours has been called an era of apathy and mediocrity—but these are by no means incurable maladies where our players are concerned. Only when we as coaches *accept* apathy and mediocrity as insoluble, incurable conditions do they become a reality. Just because no one else has ever challenged a given youngster to strive for excellence, whether in sports or in other phases of his life, there is no reason to assume that the youngster cannot be taught to accept such challenges, or that he/she will not welcome those opportunities for the team's sake as well as their own.

THE EXAMPLE SET BY PROFESSIONAL ATHLETES

Another of the teaching and motivational problems facing coaches today is that of overcoming the examples set in the professional leagues, where rules and techniques sometimes bear little or no resemblance to the amateur game. Examples abound: in pro basketball, dribblers are given an extra step at the beginning and end of their dribble, and if they happen to be fouled while driving toward the basket, they are given free throws even if they aren't yet in the act of shooting.[3] It's been years since linemen in pro football blocked without holding on pass plays, too, but no longer than the span in which major league shortstops and second basemen have skipped past second base before catching the other's toss and relaying the ball to first base in executing routine double plays.

Unfortunately, short-cuts of this sort, which are commonplace on the professional level, are not permitted under amateur rules, and coaches working with players at these lower levels of play often face enormous difficulty in teaching young athletes how to execute fundamentals correctly when they—the players—want to skip the fundamentals and go on to the shortcuts.

I admire professional athletes. As a coach, I fully understand and appreciate the skills and hard work that go into the making of a professional athlete. Still, from the standpoint of coaching in amateur sports,

---

[3]The "continuation" rule.

I think the pros generally set a poor example. Young players see their heroes taking shortcuts not allowable under amateur rules (and I'm not referring to cheating or playing dirty, but rather to mis-executing the fundamentals, or else failing to execute them at all), and as a result the high school or junior high coach is facing an uphill struggle in his/her coaching not unlike that of salmon swimming upstream to spawn. It's not easy to motivate youngsters to use techniques the pros don't bother with.

In so many other cases, the macho image of "lookin' good and bein' cool" is more important to players than succeeding. A young player sees a professional basketball player catching the ball one-handed at the end of his dribble before slam-dunking a layup, and the young viewer decides that that's the way the move is supposed to be executed. (He is, of course, unaware that the pro's finger span is 4 to 5 inches wider than his own.) A young player misses the rim and backboard entirely on a hook shot from 6 feet out because he won't catch the ball with both hands and control it before shooting. In a junior high basketball game, a player loses the ball out of bounds in the process of trying to dribble behind his back or between his legs although he is unguarded and the other nine players are setting up at the other end of the court. Those kinds of performances, and the thinking that motivates them, can reduce your chances of winning faster than a lead weight sinking in quicksand.

CHAPTER 3

Styles
of Motivation

Earlier, I presented the remarks of a disgruntled coach who considered motivation to be a glorified kind of cheerleading. Most coaches would agree that the coach's view is a shallow one, and that there is much more to motivating players toward giving maximum effort. Specifically, motivation encompasses at least three areas of concern to the coach: salesmanship, communication and psychological conditioning

MOTIVATION AS SALESMANSHIP

Let's face it, when you strip coaching down to its barest essentials, we coaches are selling a product: *hard work*. And just like door-to-door encyclopedia or vacuum cleaner salesmen, we face audiences ranging from wildly enthusiastic, to apathetic, to hostile toward the value of our product. Ours is a society in which a large portion of the youthful population is no longer dedicated to the idea of working hard to achieve success. As a result, no small part of our task as coaches has become that of convincing youngsters that the rewards of competition outweigh what they sometimes consider to be its disadvantages. We have to sell our players on the idea that spending part of their leisure time working hard to become skilled athletes is worthwhile, and will produce benefits that not participating in athletics will not achieve.

There are no guarantees in athletics except that, as is true in much of life, you get out of it only what you put into it—and even then you may fall short of achieving what you set out to accomplish. In this regard, it may be helpful to consider the words of President Theodore Roosevelt:

> It is not the critic that counts. . . . The credit belongs to the man who is in the arena . . . who strives valiantly, who errs and often comes up short again and again . . . who, at the best, knows in the end the triumph of high achievement, and who at worst, if he fails, at least fails while daring greatly, so that his place shall never be with those cold and timid souls who know neither victory nor defeat. (Cited in Lombardi, 1973, p. 16)

MOTIVATION AS COMMUNICATION

Selling your program to players is undeniably important. Still, salesmanship alone will not sufficiently meet a coach's motivational needs. Salesmanship is, at best, one-way communication. If a coach's program of motivation is to be effective, he must provide a setting in which players can learn to relate to their teammates and coaches as well. This relationship is not merely players talking together, nor is it a matter of players and coaches tolerating each other. It is a matter of *caring*, of *sharing*. Genuine communication does not require words; it grows out of a mutual sense of concern for others.

The coach's role in this process is to provide a setting in which players are urged to care about their teammates. A team is like a large family, and in many instances players develop the same kind of love for their teammates and coach that they have for their brothers, sisters and parents. If your players cannot bring themselves to love each other, they should at least be required to display respect for, and acceptance of, their teammates.

MOTIVATION AS PSYCHOLOGICAL CONDITIONING

Coaching in team sports is largely a matter of installing good playing habits and eliminating bad habits. Hustling is a habit; so is loafing. Seen in this light, the coach's task is to make hustling and working hard in practice and games a habit.

This is, of course, easier said than done, but a good place to start is the first day of pre-season practice. As Coach Jerry Tarkanian has pointed out, the level of intensity of your practices is established in your first day of organized practice, as is the level of your own expectations. Players are normally highly motivated in the earliest stages of pre-season practice, before the hard work, endless repetition of patterns and drills, and mounting pressure of a long, arduous season begin to take their toll. If you intend to condition your players to give their best effort consistently in practices and in games, you must: (1) communicate to your players in terms they understand exactly what you consider to be acceptable and unacceptable in terms of hustle and effort; (2) consistently reward good efforts and performances, and enforce sanctions against loafing, poor efforts or mental mistakes; and (3) initiate your program of intensity at the earliest possible stage of pre-season practice. After all, it's easier to establish good playing habits than to break players from using bad habits they have acquired.

When I first became a coach, I thought that coaching consisted of teaching fundamental skills and manipulating Xs and Os into workable offensive and defensive patterns. It never entered my mind that motivating youngsters to work hard and believe in themselves would also be a full-time task.

It is, though. Whether we like it or not, we're salesmen, communications specialists, and psychologists. It comes, as they say, with the territory.

I'm surprised, though, that more schools (especially on the college level) haven't gone to the kind of arrangement that Al McGuire had when he was coaching basketball at Marquette University. Coach McGuire was a master motivator, so he left the Os and Xs to his assistant coach, Hank Raymonds, and concentrated his own efforts on player relationships and motivation. If I were coaching on that level,

I'd seriously consider naming at least one assistant coach to deal with motivating the troops and handling player problems and relationships.

Coach George Allen's pet philosophy is that, as head coach, you should plan for every eventuality, and leave nothing to chance. Yet he admits that his Washington Redskins probably lost the 1972 Super Bowl to the Miami Dolphins because Coach Allen thought he didn't need to motivate his veteran squad for a game as important as the Super Bowl. It was a costly lesson.

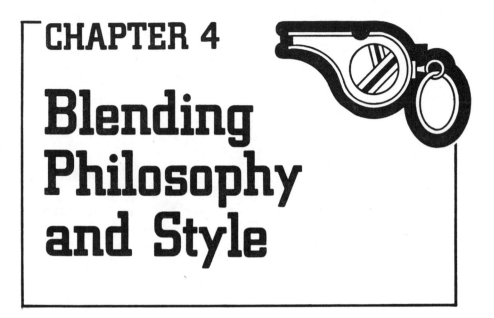

CHAPTER 4

Blending Philosophy and Style

In order for a coach to moviate his/her players, two factors must be taken into consideration: first, the coach must be willing to challenge the players in terms of individual and team goals and responsibilities; and second, the players must accept the challenge. If you're a good motivator, you already know this. And if you want to become a good motivator but are unsure how to go about the task, you can start by surrounding yourself with players who respond positively to your style of coaching.

KNUTE ROCKNE: WINNING FOR THE GIPPER

I've heard people who should know better say that young athletes nowadays are too sophisticated to respond to the old Knute Rockne "win-one-for-the-Gipper" style of motivation any more. Don't believe it for a second. If Rockne were still coaching football at Notre Dame today, he'd go out and find players who would listen to—and *believe*—that sort of approach, and he'd recruit the heck out of them, and he'd *still* beat the pants off everybody else!

We can put down Rockne's motivational talks as "corny," or old-fashioned, but that was his style; he was good at it, as good as any coach who ever wore a whistle—and you'd better believe he could make it work today, by the simple expedient of finding boys who believed what he said.

BOBBY KNIGHT: RECRUITING FOR BASKETBALL EXCELLENCE

Bobby Knight is supposed to be too intense, and too tough on his players to get many of the top basketball prospects nowadays, too—but have you checked Knight's career won-lost record lately? Many people who are opposed to Knight's philosophy and techniques keep hoping to see him fall flat on his face, but every year the wins keep piling up for Coach Knight. Every year it becomes more apparent that, regardless of whether outside observers agree with his coaching style, Knight makes it work with the people who really count: his players. How does he do it? By consciously recruiting hard-nosed athletes who will accept his style of coaching and playing as best for them.

This point is often overlooked in discussions of various coaching philosophies and styles, but a Knute Rockne, Bobby Knight, etc., isn't dealing with a cross section of the total population, or a random selection of athletes; rather the coach is dealing with a hand-picked group of athletes selected not only for their skills, but also at least in part for their attitudes toward their sport, winning, the coach and his program. Bobby Knight carefully warns prospects that, if all they are looking for is an easy four years of loafing on defense and grabbing all the glory they can for themselves on offense, they'd be better off going somewhere else to play basketball besides the University of Indiana. But if they want to work harder than they've ever worked in their lives, become better basketball players than they ever thought possible, and be in the thick of pursuit of an NCAA basketball championship constantly during their college careers, then maybe they should give serious consideration to playing basketball for Bobby Knight and the Indiana Hoosiers. Knight's intensity probably turns off some prospects, but the players who sign at Indiana tend to reflect in their play exactly the characteristics Knight is looking for—and they tend to be the kind of players who respond positively to his particular brand of motivation.

PLAYER SELECTION AND MOTIVATION

The high school or junior high coach may feel that he/she does not have such latitude in selecting players whose temperaments mirror that of the coach—which is true, but only up to a point. In the beginning stages of building a program, a coach may have trouble attracting believers, or players who accept the coach's style. As the program grows and the players' respect for the coach increases, however—and sometimes this entails waiting until his problem players graduate or quit the team—the coach will find himself with an increasing percentage of players who accept the coach's philosophy and coaching style as best for them.

Along with this, the coach should already have decided what kind of players he wants on his team. Selection of team members should be based at least in part on the basis of the players' temperaments, attitudes toward practice, willingness to entertain new ideas, and respect for the coach and their teammates. It's all part of a "weeding-out" process that virtually every coach undergoes when entering a new coaching situation or rebuilding a losing program.

The moral is, *Always let your actions be guided by a sense of what is best for your team and your program.* Surround yourself with players who think as you do, and who care about you, your program and their teammates. If this entails weeding out the players who are *not* dedicated to you, your program or the team—well, it's not an enjoyable task to consider, but it may be necessary for your own mental health as well as for your team's well-being. Problem players can age you a decade in a single season, and in the process create dissension that can tear your team apart internally.

Your responsibility and obligation are to your team and your program, not to those who by their actions or attitude could serve to tear down everything you're trying to build.

CHAPTER 5

Conversation with a Master Motivator

In concluding our introductory analysis of coaching and motivation, it should prove beneficial to consider the thoughts on the subject by a coach who is an acknowledged master at motivating young athletes. His philosophy of motivation forms a suitable framework for further anslysis of motivational philosophy and techniques.

If I ever entertained any doubts as to the importance afforded motivation by coaches, those doubts were forever dispelled in the summer of 1979 at the Mississippi State High School Athletic Association's annual convention in Jackson, Mississippi. The featured speaker in the area of basketball coaching was Jerry Tarkanian of the University of Nevada at Las Vegas, whose record of 443 wins, 57 losses, and a winning percentage of .871 over seventeen years of college coaching were unequaled in the sport. I had been fortunate enough to persuade Jerry to co-author a book on basketball with me, and I had traveled to Jackson to meet him, discuss the book with him and listen to his lectures on basketball.

I found Coach Tarkanian to be incredibly knowledgeable about

47

basketball—not surprisingly—but I was also impressed with his thoughtfulness, sincerity and down-to-earth manner. It was easy for me to see why on so many occasions even so-called "problem" athletes have responded positively to Jerry's personality and unique brand of motivation.

We were discussing a variety of basketball-related subjects in my hotel room when suddenly Jerry looked at his watch, rose, said, "I have to go now. Steve Sloan (Duke University's head football coach) is going to be talking on motivation in five minutes," and he left. I shouldn't have been surprised, though. Jerry explained that he knew Sloan to be a fine coach as well as an outstanding motivator, and that his—Jerry's—first great lesson in motivation came from another football coach, at Redlands (Calif.) High School in Jerry's fourth year of coaching. But let's have Jerry tell us about it as he explained it to me:

It seemed like our football team always had outstanding records every year, even though our kids weren't as big or as fast as the kids from some of the other, larger schools we played in the area.

Every Monday, the area coaches would get together to discuss their upcoming games on the radio, and one by one they would get up and tell how their 220-lb. linemen were being considered for All-State honors, or how they had a flock of backs running the forty in 4.5 or better. When it was our coach's turn to speak, he'd get up and talk about how little and slow his kids were, and by the time he was finished you'd be convinced that there was absolutely no way he could survive, let alone *win*, the game that week. And then Friday night his skinny, slow-footed little team would go out and whip those 220-pound linemen and 4.5 sprinters by 42–7, or something like that. Naturally, I was interested in finding out how he did it, so I asked him if I could go with the team on their next road trip. He said Sure, he'd be glad for me to go along.

The players were already dressed out and on the bus when I arrived. As I climbed aboard, the first thing I noticed was the utter silence. Nobody was talking, not even the coaches. The silence hung in the air like a heavy fog. I can't remember anyone on the bus saying a single word until we arrived at our destination.

When we pulled into the parking lot and parked the bus, the coach rose, turned to the players and said, "Let's go. Get your helmets on." There was a brief flurry of activity, and then the Pop!, Pop!, Pop!, of chin straps snapping into place. It was the most impressive sound I'd ever heard. I decided then and there that *that* was the way I wanted to coach.

The players filed off the bus quietly, went out onto the field for their pre-game warmup, and then proceeded to crush another of those bigger, faster opponents our coach had assured everyone on Monday would have no trouble beating us. I think the score was 35–0, but it could have been worse.

Every since then, I've tried to incorporate those ideas into my own team's preparation for games. Every coach has to do what he thinks is best, but I've found that the idea of building quiet intensity works best for my teams. I don't like the "rah-rah!" approach in which the players try to show that they're fired up by out-yelling the opponents, or trying to initimidate them by shouting. Yelling doesn't win ball games. It doesn't put any points on the scoreboard. Anyone can yell, even the players who are going to give you no better than 40 percent effort in games.

I don't like the idea of players' talking among themselves or sitting around listening to soul music or rock 'n roll when they should be thinking about the upcoming game, either. I just don't think intensity is something you can turn on and off like a radio. The players' intensity and readiness to compete should build steadily in the hours preceding a game to the extent that, when they finally take the court, they do so in the frame of mind of soldiers going into battle. That was exactly the impression I had when I heard those chin straps popping into place years ago.

I don't want my players loose before games. I don't want them to have a casual attitude toward the upcoming game. I want their minds and bodies committed 100 percent to the task that lies ahead.

I have no desire to control my players' lives, but I do feel that at certain times I have both the right and obligation to guide their thoughts and actions toward those goals that the team is trying to accomplish. My players know that I'll work with them to the best of my ability to help them solve their personal problems off the court, but they also know that, when they walk out on the basketball court for practice or games, I demand 100 percent effort and attention to the matters at hand. I love my players, and they know it. They know I'll go as far as I can within the bounds of the NCAA's rules in working with them to straighten out their problems—but they also know that I expect them to help me solve my problems, which includes preparing my team to win basketball games.

We don't treat game days as if they were just another day in the life of a player. We try to keep the players together as much as possible on game days, beginning at about 11:00 for home games, and possibly even earlier for road trips. We let the players get together in small groups, whether watching television, playing cards, studying or just talking among themselves, until our pre-game meal.

Shortly before 4:00,[1] we get the team together and take them out for a steak dinner, and it is at this point that we begin to build the intensity that we hope will carry over into the game. We don't permit any talking by the players or coaches while they're eating. The coaches sit with the players, and follow a standard procedure during the meals: they (the coaches) eat slowly, if at all, and never more than half of what was on their plates originally. A coach will look at his food disinterestedly, and maybe push it around his plate with his fork, and finally he'll push the plate away with a sick look on his face, conveying the message that his thoughts and energies are focused on the game ahead rather than on eating. (And with me, at least, it isn't acting!)

After dinner, most of the kids generally want to stay together, but sometimes when we're on the road we'll let some of the players walk around the campus briefly, after carefully warning them not to get into trouble or tire themselves out. Most of the players, though, prefer to sit around talking quietly. We don't want any loud talking, laughing or horseplay during this period. We want them to be focusing their thoughts on the game.

When we send the players in to suit up for the game, all talking ceases except that which is absolutely necessary for game preparation. By this time, if we've conditioned our players properly, they are in a meditative mood and ready to play basketball. Their minds are completely absorbed with their individual preparations for the game.

My pre-game talk is generally businesslike and directed toward explaining one last time to each player how his individual assignments relate to team goals. I don't go in for the inspirational pregame pep talks—for several reasons: first, I'm just not that sort of person. I'm not a great speech maker; I'm a coach. Besides, I just don't think words win ball games. Players do. Preparation does. If I have my kids ready to play the game, they won't need a fiery speech to arouse them to their best efforts—and if I haven't prepared them adequately, no amount of talking in the world is going to make up for it.

Instead, I might remind the players of how hard they've worked to get where they are, and point out that none of it would have been possible without constant hard work. I agree with Bud Wilkinson that you've got to be afraid of losing what you've worked so hard to attain, or else nobody is going to work hard enough to avoid losing. So I'll ask the players how they like the idea of losing to a team that

---

[1]For an 8:00 game.

hasn't worked as hard, or prepared as thoroughly, as we have. I work my players extremely hard in practices, so they usually see the logic behind my words. And if they have worked hard in practice—which they usually have—they are less inclined to slack off in games, where their greatest efforts receive the greatest rewards.

And that's my approach to motivation. I don't consider motivation to be a matter of getting players "up" for games; instead, I see it as a continuing process of conditioning players to automatically give their best efforts whenever they are out on the basketball court, whether in practice or in games.

I don't have all the answers about motivation, but I don't think anyone else has all the answers, either. That's why I've always been willing to listen to anyone, anywhere, who might have better ideas about how to motivate your kids. Because if you can't motivate, you'll never be a successful coach.

My intention in including the previous section is not to imply or infer that Coach Tarkanian's techniques are somehow superior to those of other coaches, although Tark is widely acknowledged to be an effective motivator. Jerry is the first to admit that his efforts have fallen short of reaching some of the boys he's coached over the years. Still, his open-mindedness and willingness to entertain new ideas deserve attention. Jerry's concept of motivation as an ongoing process of trying to reach his players and find out what motivates them to strive toward optimum performance is not unique. Coaches everywhere are vitally interested in reaching unreachable stars, if you'll pardon the pun. Jerry Tarkanian feels that any player can be motivated if he/she is loyal to you, your program, and his/her teammates. In Tark's scheme of things, the only "bad" kid is one who has no sense of obligation to the coach, the program or the team.

In Part Two, we'll explore twenty four guidelines for successfully motivating players toward their best performances, whether in practices or in games.

PART TWO

TWENTY-FOUR
MOTIVATIONAL
GUIDELINES
FOR COACHES

CHAPTER 6

Motivation and the Coach

SEVEN GUIDELINES FOR THE COACH

1. Be motivated yourself.

Examples start with the coach. If you hope to motivate your players to work hard, your own efforts should reflect your commitment to hard work. More important, the level of your commitment will determine the commitment, involvement and concern of everyone else in your program. Your enthusiasm will be transmitted to your players through your every action.

You have no more right to expect your players to be self-motivated without the example of your own motivation and hard work than you have to expect them to work themselves into shape to face the demands of competition through rigorous physical conditioning on their own.

The statement that "examples start with the coach" also refers to the relationship between the head coach and his/her assistant coaches as well. Coach George Allen (1973, p. 76) stated that he has never known of a single coaching situation in which the assistant coaches outworked the head coach. If the head coach is lazy, the assistant coaches are going to be even lazier: after all, why should they—the assistant coaches—go beyond the call of duty to make a lazy head coach look good?

2. Think positively.

If you already have a successful, thriving program, you have every reason in the world to think positively. If you have not yet reached that level of achievement, your thoughts and actions must be guided by a dream of what you hope to accomplish, and by belief in your ability to build such a program in your present coaching situation. That dream, an indomitable spirit and an unswerving dedication to making that dream a reality will provide the incentive to carry you through whatever hard times lie ahead.

Every coach should undergo at least—or better, at *most*—one losing season. It's a humbling experience, and certainly not an enjoyable one, but it can serve several valuable purposes: among other things, losing will point out, in the most graphic terms imaginable, exactly where your weaknesses as a coach (as well as those of your players) lie; it will also test your will and your commitment to coaching. If you ever harbored illusions of coaching as a glamorous profession in which all you do is let a group of highly skilled athletes scrimmage every day while you sit back and watch the victories roll in, there's nothing like a losing season to bring you back to reality.

You can't give up, not if you intend to remain in coaching. You can't quit, and you can't let your players give up. You must consider defeats as temporary setbacks from which you can learn. You can, and will, learn more from the games you lose than from the games you win.

3. Be flexible. Don't be afraid to use new or different approaches to motivation.

Use whatever technique will reach your players. The chief criterion for gauging the effect of your motivational efforts and techniques is *success:* if it works, use it. If it doesn't work, forget it.

How do you know beforehand if a given technique or method will work? You don't. You just keep trying until you find something that works.

The good motivator will try virtually anything ethically and morally acceptable to reach his or her players. As a result, the good motivator is likely to make more mistakes than the coach who, for whatever reason, does not try to motivate his or her players. In the final analysis, not trying to motivate players is a far more serious mistake than committing errors in trying to motivate players. You can always learn from your mistakes, as long as those mistakes result from an honest effort to improve yourself or your team.

4. Control yourself.

If you expect controlled performances from your players, you must retain enough self-control in pressure situations to deal with problems rationally. If you feel compelled to use profanity—and hopefully you won't—use it sparingly for its shock value, and not as a way of life. One high school girls' coach used every four-letter word he could think of in bawling out his team in the dressing room at halftime, and found out later to his dismay that two of the players' mothers had been in the restroom adjoining the varsity girls' dressing room when he began his tirade. Too embarrassed to make their presence known to the coach, the mothers listened in shocked silence— but they were not silent the next morning when they and other parents came to the principal's office demanding that the coach be fired!

A related problem can sometimes be averted by the coach's speaking distinctly. A coach called his boys "a bunch of quitters" during a halftime talk, and one of the players later complained to his parents that the coach had accused them—the players—of being homosexuals.

While the use of profanity by the coach may or may not be accepted or tolerated by administrators, parents, players and fans, the use of physical force, whether by touching the players or by using implements such as paddles, is NEVER acceptable. I was told of a basketball coach who supposedly used his belt to inspire his high school girls to greater efforts whenever they were behind at halftime. (In football, twisting players' face masks and hitting players with whistles are probably the most common offenses.)

Physical violence as used by coaches has no place in sport. When a coach touches a player in anger, it becomes difficult to justify the activity as sport, or a game. Disciplined performance is necessary for success in team sports, but that discipline should never be physical in the sense we're discussing here. A coach should never resort to corporal punishment (paddling) or touching his/her players in anger.

It's easy to lose control of yourself momentarily in the heat of contests. Pressure situations do not always bring out the best in people, and coaches are no exception. Hasty words spoken in times of duress are often regretted, and the coach who is guilty in this regard should be willing to apologize to individual players, and to the team as well, if necessary. Willingness to apologize for one's mistakes is not just a sign of maturity; it's also a sign of respect for one's players.

5. Don't cheat or look for shortcuts to success in your coaching.

If you take shortcuts or continually avoid hard work, your assistant coaches and players will, too. As was pointed out earlier, the level of a team's performance is *always* set by the head coach.

More important, every coach should understand that there are no shortcuts to success, no magic techniques known only to a few select coaches that will ensure highly skilled, highly motivated players and teams. The best motivators among coaches are, always have been and always will be, those coaches who have worked hardest to motivate their players.

Concerning motivation, probably the worst decision a coach can make is to expect his/her players to be naturally as highly motivated as he/she is, without the coach's constantly trying to reach them via external motivation. Motivation is as important a part of any coach's game plan as offensive or defensive preparations. You can ignore it to whatever extent you wish, but your team is likely to enter competition unprepared by just that much.

This is not overdramatization, either. One cannot overstate or overestimate the effect of motivation (or lack of motivation) on the level of intensity of an athlete's performance.

6. Be organized.

Organization is itself a form of motivation. Players—especially young players—want and need the kind of guidance, leadership and professionalism that is evidenced in coaches' efforts to organize their practices and program. Practice organization and attention to detail convey to your players in terms more vivid than you could ever express in words your concern for your program.

(A lack of organization can be economically costly, too. When I began a two-year sabbatical from coaching in 1979, our school had a total of 28 junior high and B-team girls' basketball uniforms; when I resumed coaching in 1981, we had a total of two jerseys and three pairs of trunks for those teams. And I've known coaches to order and give out 25–30 pairs of shoes for players during tryouts without even keeping accurate records of who received and paid for his or her shoes.)

Good organization is a habit. It's a cop-out to attempt to excuse away poor organization and administration in your program by saying "I'm just not an organized person." Good coaches are always good administrators, at least, as far as their own programs are concerned. They can't afford not to be.

7. Talk with swimming and track coaches about motivation.

Anyone who can motivate youngsters to get up at five o'clock every morning to swim 5–7 miles has to know something about motivation. And although the hours of practice may not be as severe (or as tedious) in track as in swimming, it still takes a great deal of motivational ability to build a successful cross-country or track and field program.

If you're having trouble with your own motivational program, talk with the swimming or track coaches at your school, or at other schools. If there are any secrets to motivating youngsters that the rest of us don't know about, the swimming and track coaches are probably the ones who have them.

The reader is reminded, however, that the athlete's personality may be as great a factor in his/her willingness or desire to endure the hardships of training as the coach's motivational efforts. It may well be that some individuals with a high degree of self-motivation are impelled toward participation in such demanding physical activities as swimming and track and field, regardless of the coach's ability to motivate.

Still, no such relationships have been proved or disproved, and it certainly would not hurt to talk to the swimming and/or track coaches at your school. They may have solid motivational ideas to offer—but even if they don't, the experience may clarify, organize or broaden your own thoughts concerning motivation.

CHAPTER 7

The Coach and the Players

TEN MORE GUIDELINES FOR THE COACH

8. Be consistent in your relations with your players.

This doesn't mean that you have to treat all players alike; rather, it means that your players have the right to fair and equitable treatment, whether in disciplinary matters or in helping them to solve their personal problems. If, for example, you habitually lie to your players, you shouldn't, in all fairness, expect or demand honesty from them in return. Or, to use another familiar example, if you have a team rule against using alcoholic beverages or drugs, will your punishment of violators be consistent regardless of whether the offender is a third-string player or an All-America performer?

If you cannot be consistent in your administration of a given rule, you should discard the rule entirely. If you cannot be up front, open and honest with your players, or if you break rules yourself or show favoritism, you should not expect to develop an atmosphere of mutual trust and respect among your players.

You spend a great deal of time with your athletes in the course of a school year; during that time, you'll have plenty of opportunities to show your concern for your players' well-being. You should be willing and ready to work with each of your players individually, whether in improving skills or solving personal problems. Gary Shaw's book *Meat On The Hoof* describes in graphic detail the frustrations of a seldom-used college football player who never achieved the respect or confidence of his coaches. It is not a pleasant book to read.

A coach lets his players vote for team captains, then counts the votes himself and announces the players' choices, which always just happen to coincide exactly with his own selections. And at the end of the year, the players vote again, this time for Most Valuable Player, Best Defensive Player, Best Offensive Player, Most Improved, etc., with the winners receiving trophies that already had the players' names engraved on them before the vote was taken.

Youngsters are smarter than we sometimes give them credit for being. We as coaches would be wise to remember Abraham Lincoln's advice:

> If you once forfeit the confidence of your fellow citizens, you can never regain their confidence and esteem. It is true that you may fool all the people some of the time; you can even fool some of the people all the time; but you can't fool all of the people all the time.

9. Avoid forming hasty (or permanent) negative opinions of players.

A coach cut a sixth-grader from her junior high girls' basketball team during tryouts because she thought the girl was mentally unprepared to play—the girl constantly walked when she was supposed to be running, and laughed whenever she made a mistake or missed a shot. The coach had to cut three players to trim the squad down to fifteen players, so this girl was the first to go.

The youngster waited until she was a ninth-grader before she came out for basketball again. By this time, the coach had moved on and was no longer coaching at the school. The girl, now obviously a prospect, averaged nine points per game as a freshman, and by her junior season she averaged fifteen points per game. But how much better might the girl have been if her coach hadn't given up on her when she was a sixth-grader?

No matter how we slice it, our job as coaches always involves taking chances. A youngster trying out for the team for the first time is a caterpillar that may turn out to be a moth or a butterfly. You never know. Attitudes sour or improve with age. It's all part of the risk. But we must be aware that we're not the only ones affected by our decisions. And sometimes those decisions come back to haunt us.

10. Don't make the mistake of trying to treat all players alike. Study your players. Find out whom you can push and who requires pulling.

Regardless of what anyone says, players are not alike, and you should not treat them as if they are. Their motivations as well as their personalities vary widely. Some players thrive on praise and compliments; others react as if a compliment is a signal that it's all right for them to stop hustling. Some players need the incentive of sharp criticism to stimulate them; other players fall to pieces at the first hint of negativism on the coach's part. If you study your players individually, you'll learn what motivates them best.

For coaches who need help in assessing the motivational needs of their players, assessment instruments have been developed by sport psychologists in recent years. Three such instruments are Morton's Sport Competition Anxiety Test (SCAT), Nideffer's Test of Attentional and Interpersonal style (TAIS), and the Athletic Motivation Inventory (AMI) developed by Tutko and Ogilvie.

The most popular of these instruments has been, of course, the Athletic Motivation Inventory. AMI measures, via nearly 200 multiple-choice questions, the level of eleven separate personality components: aggressiveness, coachability, conscience development, determination, drive, emotionality (the ability to handle emotions), leadership ability, mental touchness, responsibility, self-confidence, and trust.

In terms of attention and discipline, the coach should take pains to treat every player the same. He should treat them fairly, and try to divide his attention among them equally away from the court or playing field. A smile, a friendly hand on a shoulder—these small personal attentions are necessary at least occasionally to reinforce players' sense of belonging and identity on the team. Many potential problems can be avoided, or solved before they become serious, if the coach's off-court relationship with the players is warm, honest, fair and equitable.

11. Never be too busy to listen to your players.
Communication is a two-way street.

The day is largely past when coaches can get away with treating players like "meat on the hoof." More and more, players are expecting—or demanding—that coaches be concerned about them as human beings as well as players.

If a coach is going to demand 100 percent effort from the players on the court or playing field, the players deserve the same kind of commitment from the coach, both on-court and in their personal lives as well. Genuine concern for the players' well-being should not be confined to the gym or playing field.

If, for example, you're not concerned about your players' education as well as their athletic development, you're short-changing them and confusing priorities.

When a player has a problem, the coach should be willing to talk with him or her about it, and give the player a chance to talk it out. Sometimes, all a youngster needs is an adult to give him a loving pat on the back that says "I care," and to listen when the youngster needs someone to talk to.

12. Always be on the lookout for potential team leaders.

Provide opportunities for players to assume leadership roles.[1] Peer pressure is normally a powerful motivating force—more powerful, in fact, than pressures exerted by the coach. Team leaders can also act as go-betweens in gauging team mood, alerting the coach to problems involving team members, and occasionally in dealing with their teammates' problems.

Leadership is an elusive quality. Good team leaders can simplify your coaching task enormously.

13. Regardless of how hard you drive your players,
treat them with dignity and respect.
Don't rob them of their pride.

A baseball coach kept a clumsy, unskilled player on his team "for laughs," as the coach put it, to keep practices loose. It didn't take the player long to figure out that he was the joker in the deck, and he

---

[1]For further discussion of leadership, the reader is referred to Chapter 10, pp. 97–99 and Chapter 15, p. 146.

managed to accept his role without bitterness. Still, one wonders at the effect on the player, and on the team as well, of keeping a player on the squad for no better reason than to laugh at him.

14. Appeal to players' pride.

As was explained earlier, pride grows out of a sense of previous accomplishment. Winning builds pride—but seen in other terms, winning is merely a goal to be achieved, and there are other goals to be accomplished that can build pride, such as those outlined in Point #22.[2] If players take pride in their performance, the coach can appeal to that pride in motivating the team and individual players toward optimal performances. If you've worked your players hard in practice, for example, you should remind them of it when their game performances begin to lag.

15. The best motivator is love.

If you treat your players like merchandise or means to an end and nothing more, their commitment to you and your program likely will not extend very far. Coaches and athletes in the professional sports may view athletics as a business, and certainly the economics of intercollegiate athletics qualifies it as Big Business as well; still, youngsters need guidance and a sense of belonging that grows out of a coach's personal and professional behavior toward his/her players. Many coaches prefer not to become involved in the personal lives of their players. Increasingly, though, coaches are being required to deal with problems in their players' personal lives which affect their on-court performances—and this is as it should be.

Young people need adult guidance and small touches of concern and attention that make a team seem like a family. Without this kind of atmosphere—which cannot arise without the coach's active involvement—youngsters may become cynical or apathetic, or turn to drugs or alcohol to find meaning in their lives. (Drug abuse, anti-social behavior, crime and the like do not necessarily result from coaches' impersonal relationships with players; still, coaches sometimes can avert these kinds of problems by providing ingredients such as love or a sense of belonging that may be missing from their players' lives. We as coaches owe our players that much.)

---

[2]Pp. 71–72.

Too, the coach whose players believe in and support the coach and his program is going to have a natural bond of affection for his players. A sense of shared commitment always yields this kind of relationship. You can't help but love players who believe in you and your program wholeheartedly, and share your enthusiasm for the sport you've dedicated a large portion of your life to. And let me tell you, friend, if you find (or already have) a program like that, where the players can't wait to get back on the court or playing field again after practices and games are over, and where the coach and players genuinely care for and about each other—well, the motivation takes care of itself.

If you've ever been part of such a program, whether as a player or a coach, you'll probably agree that that's the way sports ought to be. And it can be that way, too. Building that kind of program takes a great deal of hard work, but it's well worth the extra effort.

16. If you are a male coach who coaches girls or women, do not, under any circumstances, permit yourself to become sexually or emotionally involved with your players.

Your proper role may be that of a boss, or counselor, or father-figure, but it should *never* be that of a lover. Beyond the problems of possible pregnancy and violent community disapproval, such behavior is both professionally unacceptable and morally reprehensible. No coach worthy of the title would take advantage of his players' vulnerability in such a manner.

17. Never offer players money, gifts or material incentive for performances.

Money is, of course, a powerful motivator; however, in addition to the illegality of playing for pay in amateur athletics, the coach who pays players is as much as admitting that he or she cannot motivate them in conventional ways. And if such is the case, the program is in deep trouble anyway.

Once you've motivated players with monetary bribes, you'll never reach them any other way.

CHAPTER 8

Motivation and the Program

SEVEN FINAL GUIDELINES FOR THE COACH

18. Start your motivational program early.

Two days before playoffs begin is a bit late in the season to start trying to motivate your players toward giving a total effort physically and mentally. Many coaches begin their motivational campaigns before school starts, by cleaning up the gym or playing field, repainting where necessary, putting up inspirational posters, signs and slogans, etc., and generally making things more attractive for the players' arrival. Additionally, some coaches write personal letters to their returning players and their parents during the summer, outlining individual and team goals for the upcoming year, offering encouragement, and subtly reinforcing in the players' minds the value of their places on the team.

On another level, starting the motivational program early also refers to recruiting, and keeping, young players interested in your sport. The "Tiger Tykes" program at Louisiana State University,

67

"Bama Bouncers" in Alabama, and the "Junior Pros" program in Kentucky are excellent examples of statewide basketball programs for youngsters. Anyone can start such a program in virtually any sport on a local level. It takes a great deal of hard work to initiate such a program—but then, virtually everything of value in life requires hard work.

If you're a varsity coach and no feeder system exists to bring young players into your program at the junior varsity or junior high level (or even earlier), by all means use every resource at your disposal to create opportunities for participation at those levels. In most situations you can, through diligent effort, find coaches for those teams, whether within your school or in the form of community volunteers. And if the coaches are not particularly knowledgeable about your sport, you can and should work closely with them, teaching and encouraging them and providing resources and information at their disposal.

19. Build your program around players you can motivate—that is, around players who are loyal to you, their teammates and your program.

Normally, this process is time-consuming, which explains why so many outstanding coaches undergo losing seasons in their first season or two at new schools, and why coaches generally expect to take 3–4 years to build a winning program where none existed previously. (Collegiate freshman-eligibility rules have alleviated this problem to a large extent on that level of play—assuming, of course, that the coach is able to recruit high-calibre freshmen—but the coach entering a new situation is likely to face the animosity of returning upperclassmen who may either dislike the new coach's methods, resent his having replaced a coach they liked, or simply fail to become motivated to give the kind of physical or mental effort the coach feels is necessary to build a winning program.)

It is advisable to limit your squad to those players who can contribute to the team's success, whether by virtue of their skills or their positive attitudes, rather than filling out your team with unskilled players with questionable attitudes simply to have a full complement of players on the team.

UCLA's legendary John Wooden has said that probably the most difficult problem he encountered during the twelve years in which he was winning ten NCAA basketball championships was controlling morale among the marginal players on his squads. These players, all of whom had been star athletes in high school, were unused to the reduced playing time they were receiving. Sometimes they were dissatisfied with their lot even though their teams were winning at a rate unknown before or since in college basketball. Coach Wooden was a good enough coach to handle these kinds of problems, but he confesses that they gave him no end of worries at the time. As a result, he has stated that he prefers to have only a limited number of outstanding players on his team at any given time, under the theory that too much of a good thing truly *is* too much.

And even though most coaches aren't burdened by an overabundance of outstanding players, the problem is a fairly common one, particularly among teams with players who are roughly equal in skills.

20. Stress total effort and striving for excellence in everything you do. Motivate on a short-term basis for physical effort and mental concentration, and on a long-term basis for those same qualities plus higher skill levels.

No amount of motivation is going to complete passes, cause field goal attempts to be successful, get basehits or score goals in soccer or hockey if the players are incapable of executing the skills involved. Thus, short-term goals are likely to be more successful when they involve physical effort, mental concentration and striving for excellence. Skills involving complex neuromuscular coordinations (e.g., shooting a basketball, hitting a baseball, passing a football, etc.) are developed over relatively long periods of time, and thus serve better as long-range goals.

21. Set high, but realistic, expectations for yourself and your team.

Every athlete should be regularly exposed to the thought that *you can do more than you think you can*. We've all seen or heard of examples in this regard. A 95-lb. mother lifts the front end of a 3,000-

lb. automobile off the ground to free her child trapped under a wheel. A blind person teaches figure skating and performs exhibitions regularly. An athlete largely paralyzed from the neck down as the result of a swimming accident becomes an accomplished painter, holding the brushes with her teeth.

You try to teach a youngster a new skill, and he/she is likely to either try it once, awkwardly and unsuccessfully, or else not try it at all, complaining that "I can't do it that way." *Well, of course you can't,* you reply. *You couldn't walk the first time you tried, either.*

I can't. I'll try. Two phrases with a world of difference between them. While goals and expectations should be realistic, they should be challenging enough to give your players the opportunity to discover that they can do more than they thought they could.

Too often, we as coaches either set our expectations too high for our teams (in which case the fall from grace may be shattering to team morale), or else we set our expectations so low that our teams never gain any sense of accomplishment or begin to approach their potential. Of the two errors, the latter is far more serious, since a lack of challenge can quickly lead to boredom and disinterest. (A coach whose basketball team was 2–8 going into the Christmas break told me, "I've already accomplished what I set out to accomplish this year." Presumably, his 4–17 record at season's end made him doubly proud of his efforts.)

It's not unreasonable to expect your team to improve as the season progresses, through a combination of hard work and sacrifice. When a team begins to slide downward toward a mediocre or even terrible season, some coaches lower their expectations to the point where further progress is well nigh impossible for the team. Granted, it's not easy to coach a losing team without suffering a drop in team morale—but thousands of coaches do just that every year.

It's important to set high, but at least partially attainable, expectations for your team. Your players don't really want to let you down, and (in my experience, at least) they won't give up unless you give up on them. You won't lose control of your team as long as the players feel that they are working toward something. You may have to alter your expectations a bit from winning—a concrete goal if ever there was one—to something less easily definable but equally important, such as *improving with every game.* But since you as coach are the only party qualified to know when and where improvement has occurred, *your* expectations will tend to define your team's success or failure in the players' eyes.

22. Outline goals clearly.

Goal-setting is an important part of motivation. If your goals are unclear, your players will not know what they are being motivated to do. (A college coach called time out near the end of a closely contested game, and when the players were gathered around him in the huddle, listening expectantly for whatever game-winning advice he had to give them, he looked up at them and said, "I want you boys to go back out there and *win!*")

A knowledgeable and experienced coach once told me,

> I've never believed in setting goals for players in terms of winning games. I want it in the back of their minds, of course, but I want them to focus their thoughts on more concrete goals. I've talked about winning sometimes in the course of games, but not as a goal.
>
> For example, if you're a point or two ahead with just a few seconds remaining in the game and you have a player at the line shooting free throws, you might call a time out and tell the player not to worry, that your team is going to win the game anyway, regardless of whether we make—not he or she makes—the free throws. In this case, you're trying to relax the player by making the free throws seem less important. But you don't have to tell a player that your team needs the free throws to win. The player knows that already, just by checking the scoreboard.
>
> Besides, you don't want to put the pressure of winning or losing on one player's ability to execute a skill perfectly under pressure if it can be avoided. That's the best way I know to undermine players' confidence in themselves or their teammates.

Instead of talking about winning, many coaches prefer to stress playing with intensity and mental toughness. Skills can always fall short in any given game, but losses are always harder to take when your players didn't play hard enough to win. Lapses in skills are human, and thus are more easily forgivable than lapses in hustle or concentration.

Concrete goals are easily understood by players. Thomas Sheeran (1976, p. 14) lists three advantages of setting specific achievement goals: each player's goals become highly personalized, desired outcomes are specified with exactness, and the athlete is required to formulate definite plans toward accomplishing those goals.

A close friend swears that, when he was playing high school football, he heard the following exchange between his head coach and one of the players:

"Hatcher, go in there and *get tough!*"
"Sure, coach, what's his number?"

Players aren't mind readers; you have to tell them what you want them to do, and in terms so explicit and simple that even the slowest player understands what you're talking about. That's good teaching—and coaching—technique.

23. Don't take all the fun out of playing the game.

It should be rather obvious by now that coaches and players are guided by different motivations. In many situations, winning games means job security for the coach, and losing means getting fired—which tends to bring a sense of urgency to the coach's efforts. Players, on the other hand, may view the game as just that—as no more than a game, or as an enjoyable recreational pursuit. Somewhere between these extremes lies a happy medium.

Having fun should not be the goal of daily practices. The role (and function) of practice is to prepare players to compete, not to provide players with a pleasant, relaxing way to spend a few hours every afternoon. Preparing for competition is seldom fun for athletes in the conventional sense of the word *fun*; that is, it normally involves great outlays of physical and mental effort, whether to expand or maintain players' strength, endurance and/or concentration levels. If (or when) players ever reach a point where they no longer are willing to accept the rigors of training—if they no longer enjoy practicing or competition—further motivation is virtually impossible to achieve.

The word *fun* means different things to different people, and in different situations. To players unused to discipline or hard work, *fun* may involve having loose, unstructured practices in which players are largely free to do as they wish, including not practicing at all unless the mood strikes them. To other players—those who have been properly conditioned psychologically—*fun* is a sense of enjoyment and personal satisfaction derived from improving skills, indulging in competitive drills and scrimmages, and pursuing team goals. The prudent coach will stress this latter kind of thinking among his or her players.

The coach can make practices more enjoyable for players by switching drills occasionally to alleviate the tedium of daily routine, by adding new and challenging drills, or by taking time out occasionally to indulge in nonessential activities or competitive drills which are related to their sport—for example, by holding slam-dunk or ball-handling contests in basketball, punting or placekicking contests in football, or home run contests in baseball. Players are always grateful for these kinds of breaks in daily practice routine—and their gratitude is likely to translate into greater enthusiasm for *all* of the drills and activities in your daily practices.

24. Avoid public actions or statements that can serve to motivate your opponents.

Perhaps the best argument for calling off the dogs when you have a team beaten is the strange way running up the score on opponents can come back to haunt you. The Houston Cougars beat Rice, 63–0, in football in 1979; a year later, an aroused Rice squad turned the tables to defeat Houston, 35–7. And you'd better believe the Owls would have poured it on even more if they had been able to! The desire for revenge is one of the most powerful motivating forces available to coaches. That's why the legendary Adolph Rupp, whose Kentucky basketball teams once beat an opponent 22 times in a row over an 11-year period, took pains to describe that team's coach as "the smartest basketball coach in America," although the team in question had suffered through fourteen consecutive losing seasons. It's practically an honor to be beaten by a living legend who tells everybody that you're the smartest coach in basketball. Coach Rupp had that particular opponent in his hip pocket, and he was not going to risk that status by offending anyone even remotely connected with that school's basketball program.

Aside from humiliating opponents by running up astronomical scores against them, probably the greatest source of annoyance to opponents is a player's or coach's downgrading or belittling them publicly, as in talking to newspaper or television reporters. It isn't terribly difficult to motivate your players against opponents who have publicly announced their hatred for you.[1]

---

[1] Following this line of reasoning, we might wonder if it was Michigan's coaches who called a halt to the traditional practice at that school of referring to arch-rival Michigan State as "Moo U."

There may in fact be a great deal of intense rivalry, or even genuine dislike, between two teams, but few if any coaches want their players to describe the intensity of their feelings to the press or other media. It just isn't done. Most coaches routinely warn their players about saying anything to reporters that can be construed as criticism of the opponents. Talking doesn't win games, but as every coach knows, it can lose them.

No useful purpose is served by belittling opponents publicly after having beaten them convincingly; in fact, such actions diminish the importance of the winning team's achievement, by subtly inferring that anyone could have done it as easily. Too, graciousness in victory or defeat shows a certain amount of class. Coaches are always trying to eliminate dumb mistakes, and certainly failing to maintain a healthy respect for opponents is a dumb mistake that can come back to haunt you.

When Bear Bryant was coaching at Texas A&M, he often complained that he was never able to sneak up on anybody because A&M's rooters, always a loud and boisterous crew, spent their time telling the next week's opponents how the Aggies were going to destroy them on Saturday. At the University of Alabama, Bear took pains to warn anyone who would listen that the upcoming opponent, whether Vanderbilt or Memphis State, was a power to be reckoned with on the scale of a Notre Dame or Southern California. Nobody believed it, of course, but Bryant wasn't going on record as telling anyone that the game would be less than a life-and-death struggle for his undermanned Crimson Tide. And after the game, Bear unfailingly told reporters how deceptive that 42–0 score was. "We didn't execute well today," Bear would say, straight-faced, overlooking the 425 yards rushing his fifteen running backs amassed, "but that was because they (the opponents) hit us so hard. They're really gonna be a fine team next year." With today's victory less than ten minutes old, Bear was already paving the way for next season's massacre.

That was one of the oldest gimmicks in Bryant's bag of tricks: you had to motivate your own team when you prepared to meet Alabama. Bear Bryant wasn't about to slip up and motivate your team for you.

PART THREE

MOTIVATIONAL TECHNIQUES

CHAPTER 9

Building Confidence, Dedication and Pride

LONG-TERM MOTIVATION: THE MOTIVATIONAL POTENTIAL OF A SUCCESSFUL PROGRAM

Virtually every successful coach considers a well-conceived, organized program of long-term motivation to be more effective and desirable than a sporadic, shotgun approach to short-term motivation. In a truly workable program of long-term motivation, the coach is *always* motivating his players, not just on game days, but in daily practices and between practices as well. He motivates through the single-mindedness and dedication he displays in his attitude toward practice and games (e.g., meticulous organization of practice schedules, game plans, scouting reports, etc.): through constantly transmitting to his players his philosophy of life, sports, and the values of competition, whether in team meetings, at practice sessions, or in individual conferences with players; and through his endless efforts to build a unified team of players who are as totally committed to the team as he (the coach) is.

77

In other words, a long-term motivational program is one in which the coach transmits—as often as possible and in as many ways as he can find—his love for his sport and his personal concern for both the team and the individual players who comprise the team. No opportunity should be considered too small, no player too unimportant, to fall within the scope of the coach's endless quest for ways to teach his players to think and act as he does where the team and the sport are concerned.

If you tell your players often enough what you believe, they'll eventually become believers, too. And *that* is precisely what long-term motivation is all about.

Sermonettes—Daily Doses of Philosophy

I always have my athletes run a mile before practice begins. Every day, though, I let a different player skip the running so we can talk in my office. The players thus look forward to my talks ("sermonettes," I call them) as a way of getting out of some of the running we do at practice, and I get the opportunity to tell them again what participation in athletics means to me, what the team is all about and why it's so important to all of us. I tell the player how others in the school look up to him/her, and of the affection his/her teammates have for him/her. I stress the need for giving your best efforts all the time, and not just when you're feeling good or ready to play, but because your teammates are giving *their* best. I remind the player that he/she didn't invent pain, and that doing your best requires that you learn to take a certain amount of pain. I don't always say the same thing to every player, but I always touch on a certain facet of my philosophy of how the game should be played, what you get out of competition, and how being a part of the team means you get out of its exactly what you put into it.

Two benefits from this type of approach are that (1) over a period of time, the players learn to regard the game in a manner approximating that of the coach; and (2) even if, for whatever reason, your players do not accept your philosophy, at least they cannot use the excuse that they don't understand you.

Obviously, the "sermonette" technique can be used in addressing the entire squad as well as one player. Many coaches (myself included) do, in fact, use the first five minutes or so of practice time to talk to the assembled team, not only about the daily practice schedule, but about various bits of the coach's philosophy as well. And some of these coaches carry the process even further by using selected, easily remembered slogans and phrases to get their points across, not only in talking to the team, but later in the course of practice as well.

Once you reach the point where your players think as you do—and I'm not referring to game strategy or tactics, but to the players' and coach's basic attitudes about the level of intensity of effort at which the game should be played, and the importance of a sense of obligation and responsibility to the team—your motivational battles are 90 percent won. Once your players are won over to your way of thinking, your short-term motivation will be a snap. If, for example, the players accept your views on the values of participation, they'll accept your view of the importance of a given game or practice session. If they carry within themselves a sense of obligation to the team and its goal, they won't let you and their teammates down in games.

However, the reader should be reminded that we're talking here about long-range, and not short-term, motivation. If you take five minutes out from practice today to talk to a given player or the team, that's short-term motivation. Do it every day for an entire sport season, and then two seasons, and so on, including the time between seasons, and *that's* long-term motivation. Don't expect, then, that today's five-minute talk will change viewpoints overnight. It *may*, of course—but it probably won't. That's why it's important to have long-range motivational goals in mind when you enter a new situation.

Too, you cannot reasonably expect to reach every player with such an approach or any other. Some individuals will be forever beyond you. Losing them hurts, too. Once I talked for 2-1/2 hours to a junior trying out for my track team for the first time, telling her that, with her athletic potential, she could bypass the normal apprenticeship period and become an outstanding performer *immediately* as a distance runner if she could gradually work herself into shape and learn to accept the pain associated with competitive running. (Our Region wasn't particularly strong in terms of quality distance runners.)

Although the girl merely jogged the first day, I could tell that she wasn't nearly as enthusiastic about becoming a runner as she'd thought she was. I talked with her for an additional 1-1/2 hours the next day as well before sending her out to jog some more. She wasn't a championship prospect, but merely a kid who had been mainstreamed from Special Ed. I told her that it would be a great opportunity for her to accomplish something really important for the first time in her life.

She quit the team on the third day. And not only had she wasted an opportunity to do something meaningful in her life, but she also wasted four hours of *my* time that could have been better spent talking with youngsters who were going to stick it out. But that's the way it goes; you win some and you lose some. It always hurts to lose kids, but it's not as painful when you know you gave it your best shot in trying to reach them.

Unlocking the Doors of Response

Personally—and I base this conclusion solely on the empirical evidence of my own experience in coaching—I believe there's a key of sorts that unlocks the door to reaching inside each player—that is, that there's some special kind of underlying motivation that impels each players, and if I talk to that player long enough, I'll eventually stumble over the key to reaching that player. I don't always find those keys to every player, of course, but when I do, I can "hold that player in my hand," as Bear Bryant put it, where motivation is concerned.

For example, I coached an athlete named Clara Harden who, although only 5'2", averaged 27.3 points per game in basketball her senior year and won so many ribbons and medals and trophies in three years of Region and State track competition that one coach suggested that the Region High Point Trophy be retired to her when she graduated.

Now, you know as well as I do that players—even the best of them—are going to have "off nights" occasionally. And when everyone within a 150-mile radius is talking about how great you are, the temptation sometimes exists to slack off, even if you happen to be only 5'2". But I wasn't about to let it happen to Clara, first, because I constantly was reminding her that 27-ppg. scorers couldn't afford "off nights," and second, because I had the key to motivating her. I knew what motivated Clara. When she looked as if she was beginning to slack off, all I had to do was compliment one or more of her teammates. Clara could not stand to be out of the limelight, so whenever I began to pay more attention to her teammates than to her, she never failed to respond with performances that would knock your eyes out.

Of course, not everyone responds equally to the same motivational slant. Some players dislike being placed in the limelight; others thrive on it, as Clara did. The secret is to find out what each player responds to—normally this process involves trial-and-error—and if and when you find that secret factor, bombard them with it whenever you want to motivate them. It relates to Abraham Maslow's hierarchy of needs, which contends that all of us have basic needs which must be fulfilled. If you can tap into that system to find out what a given player needs in the way of motivation, and then gear your motivation toward creating a situation whereby giving his/her best effort fulfills that need, then you have uncovered an inexhaustible supply of motivation for that player, available whenever you need it. It's virtually a foolproof system, provided that you can keep the players in your program long enough for you to find the key that reaches them.

The most difficult period of any coach's tenure at a given school is always the first year or two, regardless of whether we're talking about building a program or motivating players.

Concerning motivation, when you enter a new coaching situation, you and the players are strangers to each other. As a result, determining what is likely to motivate them often turns out to be guesswork. As you get to know the players, you will find out what kinds of approaches are most effective in reaching them. Unfortunately, this process is largely trial-and-error, and thus time-consuming.

The longer you remain at a given school, the easier your motivation will become. In addition to the simple fact of the players' knowing you better, you will tend to attract more and more personality types into your program that are similar to, or at least compatible with, your own personality and philosophy, regardless of whether you consciously attempt to select such players. Athletes who understand and accept you and your sport philosophy normally will respond favorably to your motivational style.

Competition and Success

While great champions are always great competitors, the converse is not always true. Not every great competitor is, or can be, a champion.

We as coaches do not have it in our power to install superstar skills into players of less than superstar potential. We do, however, have it within our power to increase the level of our players' competitiveness, through the example of our own dissatisfaction with being in a subsidiary position, through the formal and informal process of imparting our philosophy to our players, and through constantly placing them in competitive situations which demand their finest efforts. As one coach tells his players, "There's no disgrace in losing; the disgrace is when you reach a point where it doesn't matter to you any more whether you win or lose."

We tend to think of successful programs as those in which victories roll in with clockwork precision and regularity. Indeed, winning *is* important in the formation of a successful sports program; still, while victories give concrete evidence of success, the level of competitiveness displayed by players throughout the program is a more reliable indicator of whether the coach's efforts to build a successful program are actually paying dividends.

According to the old saw, there are three kinds of lies: lies, damned lies and statistics. Scores are statistics, too. Thus, the truest indicator of improvement in a given sports situation is likely to be the level of comeptitiveness displayed by the team and individual players. Are they consistently blown out of games that should have been close? Do the players continue to play with the same intensity when they fall behind as when they are ahead or the score is tied?

Only you as the coach know for sure whether your team performs capably in this regard, which is precisely why *yours* is the voice the players should listen to in determining the degree of success your program is experiencing.

Winning and Success

One of all-time great basketball coach Arnold "Red" Auerbach's most famous quotes was, "Show me a good loser, and I'll show you a loser." While some have taken this to mean that Auerbach favors athletes being poor losers, I don't think he meant that at all. Rather, he meant that one should never be satisfied with losing. Satisfied players are difficult to motivate. Hungry players—in the sense of competitive tension—win championships. When they lose that competitive edge, they lose games as well.

Your first goal is to raise, by whatever means possible, the level of competitiveness displayed by your players. Your second goal is to win as many games as possible. As Reuben Frost (1971, p. 80) has pointed out, repeated successes tend to yield higher aspirations and expectations, while repeated failures tend to lower individual or team goals.

It's all a matter of *expectations*. The more you win, the more you expect to win in the future. And the more you expect to win, the harder you'll work to avoid losing. You don't have to win every game, of course, but you need to win often enough to keep your players from lowering their expectations and goals.

Seen in this light, developing a successful program refers to the process whereby accumulated successes bring about a rise in the expectations of players in your program concerning the outcome of competition. Usually, this rise in expectations is a gradual process, and, with all other factors being equal, the longer you remain associated with a program, the greater your chances will be of building, and then maintaining, a high level of competitiveness among your athletes.

SURVIVING THE FIRST YEAR

Where there is no vision, the people perish.

Proverbs 29:18

All of us as coaches carry within ourselves a vision of a better world. For most of us, that better world is made manifest, not in outrageously high salaries or a life of luxurious splendor, but in the comparatively mundane (but eminently satisfying) sense of self-realization to be achieved through the medium of athletics. A certain amount of glamor is associated with coaching—but it is not the glamor or the headlines that shape our efforts in coaching; it is the *dream*, the *vision* of what we can be, or become, that compels us. Motivation consists of communicating that vision to the young people who comprise our teams, and then convincing them that the dream is worth pursuing.

Unfortunately, not everyone shares our belief in the ultimate value of that pursuit. Some people will react to our best efforts with total indifference, others with open or scarcely concealed hostility. For a young coach entering a new situation, the latter can be a shattering experience. Nothing in your previous experience as a player or a coach is likely to prepare you for ordeals such as a series of anonymous threats or obscene phone calls, or finding that someone has let the air out of your tires or poured sand into your gas tank at home games, or thrown a brick through the front window of your home, or poisoned your dog—or, as happened to ex-Head Football Coach Bill Battle of the University of Tennessee, waking up one morning to find that someone has placed "For Sale" signs in your front yard and parked a moving van in your driveway. At such times, you may find yourself wondering why you ever went into coaching in the first place, and whether you owe it to yourself and your family to remain in the profession or find a less threatening line of work.

A Sense of Humor

One way to hang in there when the going gets rough is to have a sense of humor. Losing isn't funny, but a sense of humor can help you to endure hard times. When Bill Fitch took the job as head coach of the NBA's expansion Cleveland Cavaliers, he acquired a team that managed to win only 12 of 82 games in its first year. Fitch knew, of course, that building a winner would be a long, laborious task, but he never lost his sense of humor. Once, when addressing reporters after one of the Cavs' frequent losses during that dismal period, Fitch announced, "This is one of those nights when you wish your parents had never met."

Coach Fitch's sense of humor probably was the main reason he was able to keep his job during the dark years while Cleveland was the NBA's doormat. His humor helped to divert the fans' and owners' frustration as he quietly indoctrinated his players in his style of play and made wise use of the player draft and prudent trades to forge a playoff contender out of a team that was a laughing stock when it entered the NBA.

A sense of humor will not replace skilled coaching, of course; rather, it will supplement a coach's efforts in all other areas of his operation. The coach should not merely shrug off defeats, nor should he permit defeats to drag team morale down to the point where losing no longer matters to him or the players.

If you ever reach the point in your coaching where you just don't care any more whether you win or lose, then it's probably time to get out of coaching and find a less rigorous or demanding job. You can teach your players to care, through the example of your own die-hard determination, indomitable spirit and perseverance. But if you cannot find inner strength to continue the battle, you'll never be able to convince your players that the struggle is worth the effort.

Every coach probably is manic-depressive to a certain extent. The highs of satisfying victories, the lows of miserable defeats: we're all familiar with these situations and the incredible range of mood changes they bring. But you cannot be a prisoner to these moods; you must keep your thoughts focused on your long-range goals as well as your short-term expectations.

Referring to the bitter experience of undergoing a prolonged losing streak, one coach has said that "The only four ways of dealing with it are: quitting, suicide, drinking, or a sense of humor." Of the four, the latter—a sense of humor—is the only one which will not ultimately destroy you as a coach.

Coaching from Day to Day

Earlier, we discussed the necessity of having long-range goals, and of stressing the importance of those goals (and the process whereby their achievement is made possible) to the players at every opportunity. Yet this is only half the battle: the other half consists of keeping the players in your program as you set about the task of making changes that will lead to improvement in the team's attitude and performances.

At this point, then, we should consider an important concept: *every day you can keep your players from quitting is a day farther from quitting in the future.*

An athletically-built sophomore came out one day for my track team. The other girls were jogging five laps around the football field—we didn't have a track—as part of their warm-up exercises, so I suggested that she wait until they came around again and finish jogging with them. After less than 1-1/2 laps, the girl collapsed onto the grass, crying, gasping for breath and holding her side. "I've got to quit," she said as I approached her. "I'm supposed to have an operation on my appendix next week." I shrugged my shoulders, not knowing what to say. She rose and slowly walked away. She never came back, and to my knowledge she still hasn't had that operation.

I'm not blaming the girl: I know exactly how she felt when she "hit the wall" of endurance pain. But I don't blame myself, either. She never gave me or herself the chance to stretch herself toward the limits of her potential.

One Day at a Time

Learning new skills (or improving old ones), breaking bad habits, learning to execute patterns correctly and with proper timing, getting in shape for the rigors of competition—all of these require time and effort to become natural to players. Just as you cannot reasonably expect young, inexperienced players to properly execute complicated patterns involving precise timing after only one or two practice run-throughs, you should not expect those same players to give what you consider to be 100 percent effort unless you constantly tell them what such an effort entails—and even more important, remind them of why they are working so hard. You have to constantly give new players (and veterans as well, in some cases) reasons for not quitting, or else they'll quit on you. You have to constantly remind them that, although it may seem otherwise to them, physical pain is not necessarily fatal, and that *everyone else on the team is suffering just as much as they are.*

Getting in shape always hurts. The only way for a runner to get in shape for track season is to run. Admittedly, the conditioning process consists of a gradual building up to competitive shape—but it still hurts. The only way to teach a boy to block and tackle in football is to have him practice blocking and tackling until he can do them correctly.

Meanwhile, the athlete is thinking to himself of all the less painful and demanding things he could be doing instead of cracking heads and going home from practice every day with a splitting headache and his ears ringing.

Thus, the coach must assume the task of constantly reminding athletes why the pain will be worth the effort somewhere down the line. To ignore this aspect of coaching is to invite diaster in the form of players quitting because they cannot supply reasons of their own why they should continue to struggle on for one more day.

Small Successes

In a truly weak situation, successes may not come in bunches. In such cases, three guidelines may be helpful:

1. *Don't base your team's success solely upon winning.* Look for ways to emphasize victory in defeat. Emphasize that you're building a foundation for future successes.

2. *Constantly point out areas of individual and team improvement to the players.* You may have to do some remarkable statistical analysis to find improvements initially, but it's worth the effort.
3. *Don't lie to the players and tell them they're doing fine when they're not.* They won't see the need for doing any better. Instead, stress the long-range nature of your team goals.

In case this fact hasn't been made abundantly clear by now, what you're trying to do here is to divert your players' attention away from negative factors (e.g., fatigue, pain, losing, etc.) toward more positive aspects of their performance such as individual and team improvement, and building pride and a sense of team purpose.

To divert players' attention away from present concerns—fatigue, pain and losing—stress long-range goals. (In this respect, one coach told me that he uses a "money in the bank" approach with his players, telling them that their hard work is like putting money in the bank: not only will it pay off later in games, but the harder they work, the more they'll have in reserve when they need it most.)

To divert players' attention away from their inability to achieve long-range goals now, stress present accomplishments, no matter how small, as positive steps toward achieving your long-range goals. Self-confidence and pride are natural outgrowths of a sense of accomplishment. When an athlete succeeds, in however small a task or goal, the resultant sense of enjoyment, pleasure, or satisfaction he/she experiences serves as a powerful motivator in increasing the chances of the athlete's striving even harder to accomplish that task and/or others in the future.

BUILDING FOR THE SECOND YEAR AND BEYOND

Initially, players tend to define success in their own terms, by whatever standards they set for themselves. And with the exception of self-motivated athletes, players also tend to set the standards for what they consider to be satisfactory performances far lower than they are actually capable of achieving, particularly when they have not performed well in the past.

Thus, your first year in a heretofore losing situation is likely to be spent teaching players to view their athletic experience from a perspective that differs broadly from what they've been accustomed to: the *coach's* perspective. Your task entails selling them on the merits of *your* view of athletics, whatever it may be, and then motivating them to work at the pace or level of exertion you prefer rather than following their own instincts.

Light at the End of the Tunnel

When you begin to build your program in a previously unsuccessful athletic situation, the light at the end of the tunnel is likely to be the dream you bring with you—and it may appear exceedingly small at times in the darkness and gloom surrounding you. Assuming, however, that you do not give in to despair, you can keep your dream alive, and you will attract a certain amount of young people who will believe in that dream because they've been looking for someone like you to inspire and lead them. They're going to tell their friends about you and your dream, and as time progresses you will find your program expanding to include a growing number of young athletes whose values are similar, if not identical, to yours. *These* are the youngsters upon whom you will base your hopes and aspirations. And because their values and outlook more or less mirror yours, they won't let you or their teammates down.

If the previous paragraph sounds like idealistic nonsense, it isn't. It merely describes the natural process whereby good coaches everywhere build their programs, working their way up the ladder of success. A day at a time. A week at a time. A month at a time. A year at a time.

Idealism comes into the picture when you start thinking it doesn't involve hard work.

The Second Season

By the time you begin your second season in a given school, the word is out and the verdict returned on the kind of person and coach you are. You haven't fooled anyone, even if you were foolish enough to try. The team knows by now exactly what you stand for, and whether it's worth the effort to play for you. You should have a small—or, hopefully, a *large*—nucleus of support for your program by now, including parents who understand what you're trying to do and respect you for it, and athletes who consider your demands acceptable if not enjoyable. Even if your support is minimal, though, it should be an improvement over your first year when no one understood what you were doing or why you were doing it.

Consider your returning players: if they didn't quit last year when they were unfamiliar with you and unused to the kinds of demands you made on them, they aren't likely to quit now that they believe in you and your system. Too, they should have gained an appreciation for the changes you've made in team attitude, and they can see the positive strides they've made both individually and as a team in terms of performance. And while their improvement may not have been as great or as rapid as you had hoped it would be, you certainly are not finished with your task of program development, and you aren't going to sit back and rest on your laurels.

You probably have young players coming into your program via the school's feeder program—which you initiated or expanded the previous year—and you shouldn't be overly concerned about any possible negative feedback from returning players affecting the newcomers. You probably lost most of the malcontents and troublemakers last season—and those who didn't quit or graduate are hardly uncontrollable, or else you wouldn't have let them come back out for the team this year.

A Haven for Believers

I've always wanted my players to consider the gym and/or athletic field to be a haven for believers, a place where they could interact with people who love and respect them. I don't want my players to be like so many people nowadays who seem to think that anything that requires dedication and hard work isn't worth the effort. I don't want my players to associate with those who think that drug abuse is the best way to find meaning in life.

The way around the problem, as I see it, is to create a team environment that is so desirable that the players prefer it to the shadowy, secretive atmosphere surrounding drug abusers or the "doing-nothing-and-going-nowhere" attitude of those who are willing to complain but unwilling to put forth an effort to change things. Such an environment, based on positivism, and on mutually shared love, loyalty and respect, is not merely an illusion perpetuated by the television show *The White Shadow*; it can be a reality on any team if the coach is willing to invest the necessary time and effort in building such an atmosphere on his/her teams.

CHAPTER 10

Rewards, Inspiration and Example

REWARDS, INCENTIVES AND INDUCEMENT

The concept of using rewards and punishment to induce changes in behavior is but one of four general theories of how people are motivated. Known as the "Pleasure-Pain Theory of Motivation," this theory holds that individuals tend to seek pleasure and avoid pain, and thus they learn by reacting to their environment. Emphasis is placed on responses which elicit either pleasure or pain. Motivationally speaking, then, we can produce changes in our players' behavior by rewarding or punishing them for their behavior. Rewards are used to motivate players to produce desired behaviors, and punishments are used to eliminate undesired behavior.

Since punishment as a motivating force will be analyzed in Chapter 11, present emphasis will focus on ways coaches can use rewards to induce players to exhibit desired behaviors.

In order to be successful, a program of positive reinforcement—rewards—must begin with an understanding on the part of both player and coach as to what constitutes desired behavior. Other principles underlying the proper use of rewards are as follows:

1. Reinforcement (the act of providing a reward when desired behavior is achieved) should occur immediately after desired behavior occurs, or as soon thereafter as possible, so the subject will learn quickly to associate the behavior with the reward.

2. In the earliest stages of learning, every instance of occurrence of the desired behavior should be rewarded. After the bond between behavior and reward is formed, it is advisable to offer rewards for learned behaviors only part of the time, lest the subject lose his/her desire to further modify his behavior or learn new skills.

3. In the earliest stages of learning, skills should be broken down into segments which are more easily mastered than the total skill. Joe Owens (1977, p. 6) used the term *positive psychology* to describe his concept of reinforcement. He stressed teaching skills in small steps, and reinforcing rough approximations of the desired skill along the way. Reinforcement is then provided as skills improve and performances more nearly reach the desired level. He pointed out, too, that learning is normally a gradual process, and the coach should not necessarily expect dramatic improvements overnight.

Intrinsic and Extrinsic Rewards

There are two types of rewards, *intrinsic* and *extrinsic*. Intrinsic, or internal, rewards are primarily mental, as in the sense of enjoyment or satisfaction to be derived from pursuing and achieving personal goals or being part of a team. When we talk about coaching being a "rewarding" profession, we're talking primarily about the intrinsic values we receive from our association with athletics.

When we talk about coaching salaries and supplements, we're talking about extrinsic, or external, rewards. (Considered on a per-hour basis, though, it's not really much of a reward for most of us.) Extrinsic rewards include recognition, earning trophies, letter jackets, etc., and receiving college scholarships or professional contracts.

Perhaps the easiest way of distinguishing between the two types of rewards, intrinsic and extrinsic, is to state that, while the coach has no direct control or involvement in the process through which his/her athletes are rewarded intrinsically for their participation in athletics, extrinsic rewards are part and parcel of the coach's obligation to the athletes in his/her program. Extrinsic rewards such as praise, affection, and publicizing an athlete's efforts should be a major concern for every coach.

THE USE OF SLOGANS

If, like most coaches, you use signs, posters, etc., as attention-getting devices and to convey your personal philosophy to your players, it is advisable to use brief slogans and phrases that are easily remembered. Thoughts that are too deep or lengthy will not be remembered or heeded.

The best motivational slogans are, as was mentioned, brief. They also catch the reader's attention, whether by the use of rhymes ("There are no gains without pains"), wit or irony ("There can't be an US without "U' ", "If you fail to prepare, prepare to fail"), or appeals to pride ("Winners never quit; quitters never win").

Many coaches compile personal collections of slogans. An excellent source for slogans is *Scholastic Coach* magazine, which from time to time publishes lists of brief motivational statements and slogans from well-known coaches and athletes in a variety of sports.

If you're going to hang slogans on the walls of your gymnasium, field house, coaches' office or dressing room, the signs or posters should be attractive, colorful, and neat. A hastily-scribbled slogan loses much of its appeal regardless of the relevance of its message.

THE EXAMPLE SET BY THE COACH

Although for one reason or another some coaches object to having to set an example for their players in their personal lives, the fact remains that our players are greatly influenced by the example we set for them in our personal and professional lives. The standards of expectation and performance that we set for our athletes are likely to be effective only insofar as we are willing to mirror those characteristics in our own behavior.

The Coach and Values

In coaching, we constantly transmit our values to our players, whether consciously or unconsciously. And while sometimes we lose players whose values differ widely from ours, most of the athletes with whom we come into contact are flexible enough in their thinking to accept our values as best, if not for them, at least for the team. Many of those players will, in fact, adopt our values into their own lives, which is probably the most important and lasting contribution we make to the youngsters who comprise our teams.

The term *building character*, long associated with athletic values, refers to the process whereby young people acquire positive values from their athletic experience. The coach who intends to be a passive observer rather than a participant in this process eventually finds that no such transfer of positive values has occurred.

Double Standards

Problems arise when the players sense the existence of a double standard of expectations and/or performance; that is, when they feel that they, and not we as coaches, are the ones who are doing all the work or making all the sacrifices. Few people in our society today will tolerate or accept double standards; athletes are no different in this regard from anyone else. If we expect our athletes to dress neatly and take pride in their appearance on road trips, to use one example, our own manner of dress and appearance should be at least as formal as that of the players, probably more so.

If we want dedicated, committed players who work hard and approach practices and games with a businesslike attitude; if we want to build pride; and if we want players who are honest and concerned with us and their teammates; we must exemplify those characteristics ourselves in our professional lives. Otherwise, we are likely to create and perpetuate the impression of a double standard of performance in which the players do the work while we sit back and watch. Every coach knows that there's more to coaching than that—but not every coach is willing to devote 100 percent of his/her time and efforts to the pursuit of excellence. That's probably what Coach Jerry Tarkanian meant when he said, "Show me a (basketball) coach who spends his spare time playing golf, and I'll show you a loser."

Commitment to Excellence

The best coaches in the business are, without exception, totally committed to excellence in their coaching. Name any highly successful coach in whatever sport you wish, and underlying his/her success you'll find an unswerving, single-mindedness of purpose and total dedication to excellence and winning.

The Coach as a Friend or Peer to His/Her Athletes

You should be concerned about your players, and you should manifest that concern both professionally and personally—but you should NOT attempt to relate to your players on a peer basis. You should NOT attempt to become "one of the kids." You should NOT solicit your players' friendship, except in the sense that a mother or father attempts to become "friends" with his or her child.

You can be as impersonal as a boss, or as concerned as a parent, without losing control of your team. But if you try to relate to your players as a teenager, you're asking for trouble. Poet Kahlil Gibran wrote concerning young people, "Their souls dwell in the house of tomorrow, which you cannot visit, not even in your dreams."

Mixing It Up with the Players

Many coaches possess superior physical skills which can be used as valuable teaching aids—for example, passing or kicking a football, shooting a basketball or hitting a baseball, golf ball or tennis ball. Personal involvement through demonstration is an excellent teaching method, as long as (a) the coach actually possesses the skills being demonstrated, and (b) the demonstration is intended to be just that, and not an attempt to make a given player look bad or to punish the player. Concerning the latter, using demonstration as intimidation or punishment, I've seen basketball coaches knock junior high players into the bleachers in simple one-on-one drills, and football coaches putting on pads to go up against football players who they thought needed to be taught a lesson or "toughened up."

I think most coaches would consider the lessons to be learned from such encounters, not only to be beneath the dignity of a professional coach worthy of the title, but also self-defeating in terms of team morale and the effects on the individuals involved.

Working Out with Your Athletes

Finally, it has been mentioned previously that, if we want our players to work hard at practice and in games, we must continually work hard ourselves. Many coaches—for example, Baseball Coach Ron Polk of Mississippi State University—spend a great deal of time in the off-season preparing themselves physically to work out with the players. Coach Polk contends that players can hardly complain about how hard the coach is working them when *he* is doing the same things he's asking them to do.

Still, the prudent coach will point out to his/her players that, whereas players' preparations for games are both mental and physical, the coach's preparations are primarily mental (e.g., devising daily practice schedules, studying the sport intensely, finding ways to improve the team's performances, and preparing effective game plans and strategies). Players should be told that the coaching task entails many areas of mental effort that may or may not result in perspiration and physical fatigue, and that no amount of wind sprints or other physical exertion on the coach's part is going to put any points on the scoreboard.

You may enjoy working out with your players; if so, then by all means do so. But don't forget to remind the players that the truly hard work you contribute to the team's success shows up in ways other than perspiration and fatigue. Players must be made to understand this important point.

USING TEAM LEADERS WISELY

Generally, we think of effective leadership as being *the ability to inspire confidence*, but it is more than that. It is also *the ability to motivate others, whether by word or deeds, toward desirable behavior.*

In sports, effective team leaders are not always superstar athletes, and superstars are not always effective leaders. Leadership ability is an elusive quality, a rare talent involving complex personality factors.

SEVEN GUIDELINES FOR IDENTIFYING AND
USING TEAM LEADERS

1. *Always be on the lookout for potential team leaders.* Don't overlook anyone connected with your teams in your search for leadership qualities. One of the most effective team leaders I ever had was a manager for one of my basketball teams.

The *best* team leaders are capable of taking charge of the team, and not merely setting an example for others to follow. Of course, you have to make do with what you have on hand, of course, but you should always be on the lookout for vocal, outgoing players who are liked and respected by their teammates.[1] (Another suggestion: be on the lookout for the players who want to take the last-second shot in basketball, or to be the one at bat with the tying and winning runs on base with two outs in the bottom of the ninth inning.)

Other desirable attributes of team leaders are: loyalty, dependability, maturity, self-confidence and poise. Still, the most important considerations are an outgoing personality and willingness to function as an authority figure as well as a member of the peer group.

2. *Provide opportunities for everyone to assume leadership roles at least temporarily.* Often, leadership qualities are found in completely unexpected sources. Even if you have excellent team leaders presently, they will graduate or play out their eligibility eventually, to be replaced by others in your program.

If you spot natural leadership qualities in young players who are not yet ready to assume such a role on a continuing basis—for example, in a freshman playing in his/her first year of varsity competition—bring the player along slowly, training him/her for a future leadership role. It is unwise to place too much pressure on an inexperienced athlete early in his/her career.

---

[1]The Athletic Motivation Inventory (AMI) developed by Drs. Thomas Tutko and Bruce Ogilvie measures, among other things, leadership qualities. For more on this test, see page 63.

3. *Don't expect (or demand) the same quality of leadership from every player who functions as team leader.* Assuming a leadership role places added pressure on an individual; not everyone reacts equally well to such pressures.

4. *Use team leaders to the fullest extent possible within the limitations of their personalities.* Peer pressure rates among the most powerful forms of external motivation. As a result, players who function well as team leaders often can be more effective than the coach in motivating teammates and dealing with minor problems that arise.

Such leaders are exceedingly rare, of course, since the act of leadership carries with it the possibility of peer disapproval, and relatively few athletes are willing and able to handle the resultant pressure. Still, this is precisely why such individuals should be used to the maximum extent of their willingness and ability to function as team leaders.

5. *It is possible to have too much leadership.* As mentioned previously, effective leaders are hard to find. If you find yourself facing the problem of "too many chiefs, and not enough Indians," you have either stumbled into Utopia, or else you have failed to organize and administer your program of team leadership properly—for example, by failure to adequately define roles.

If you have more than two team leaders, you probably should divide their responsibilities into non-overlapping areas such as offense, defense, and special teams, by classes (e.g., junior captain, senior captain, etc.), or by whatever method occurs to you as proper. At any rate, the entire team (including non-leaders) should be made aware of the extent and limits of the role played by each of the team's leaders.

6. *Don't expect your leaders to do your work for you. Work with them.* A coaching acquaintance who had just taken a job in a losing situation for the first time in his career complained:

> I can't believe it. At Thus-And-So High School (where he had coached previously), I always had at least one or two players who took charge, changing defenses whenever one defense wasn't working, and calling plays on their own to take advantage of weaknesses in the other team's defense. Here, though, I have to tell these kids when to breathe in and out. Nobody does anything on his own. I'm just not used to that sort of thing.

While it's nice to have effective leadership of the type described by the coach, it is a mistake to expect that kind of leadership on a continuing basis, particularly when entering a new coaching situation for the first time. The coach had never before had to develop effective team leadership before, and consequently he assumed (incorrectly) that leadership is a natural skill that players pick up in the process of participating in athletics.

7. *Provide incentives and rewards for players' assuming leadership roles.* As the coach in the previous example quickly learned, one cannot take leadership or leaders for granted. The act of leading is often a thankless job; thus, the prudent coach will find opportunities frequently to express his/her appreciation for the efforts of players willing to function as team leaders.

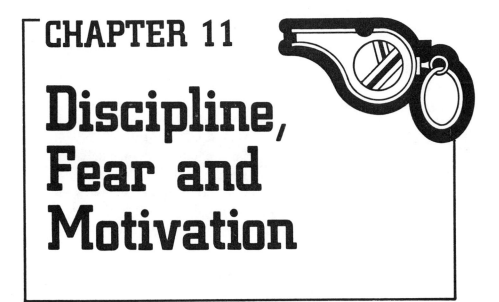

CHAPTER 11

Discipline, Fear and Motivation

THE TWO FACES OF MOTIVATION

Perhaps no word associated with coaching is more consistently misunderstood than the word *discipline*. Although connected in many people's minds with abuses of coaching authority, heavy-handed administration of arbitrarily selected rules, and an oppressive atmosphere of fear and subservience, discipline is a far less imposing ogre for most coaches and teams than the aforementioned extremes indicate. Of course, some coaches take advantage of players in their efforts to instill discipline—during the '70s, for example, when long hair was fashionable among males, a coach required his male athletes to wear crew cut haircuts as proof of their willingness to sacrifice for the team—but the number of such coaches is dwindling with every passing year.

Most coaches tend to view discipline simply as a means of maintaining order, or as a vehicle for implementing guidelines to desired individual and team behavior.

Discipline is an emotive word; that is, it conjures up mental images based on the individual's past experiences. And because discipline is associated with punishment and fear more often than it is associated with positive outcomes, it has become fashionable over the past fifteen years to consider only the negative connotations associated with the use of discipline.

Discipline as Punishment

Studies by behavioral psychologist Edward L. Thorndike and others have indicated that punishment is of limited value when used as a learning tool. Punishment is, or can be, an effective deterrent to undesired behavior, but it does nothing to indicate desired behavior. In other words, when a boy is punished for misbehavior, he may learn nothing from the experience, or he may learn what sort of behavior is *not* desired—but he will learn nothing about what type of behavior *is* desired. As a result, his future behavior is likely to be confused, erratic, and non-purposeful.

Still, whether rightly or wrongly, many people consider the threat of punishment to be an effective deterrent to undesirable behavior. Whether it rates highly as an effective motivator is a question for which each coach must find his/her own answers.

The threat of punishment can serve to motivate athletes to hustle and work harder; it cannot improve their ability to execute skills properly. In fact, it may adversely affect skills by increasing the pressure under which the skill is performed.

Discipline as Guidelines to Desired Behavior

The other view of discipline is that of guidelines to desired behavior. The disciplined athlete accepts instruction and criticism, abides by team rules, and gives his/her best effort in practice and in games. The self-disciplined player is internally motivated to pursue individual and team goals without being told to.

Disciplined athletes reflect successful program continuity. When you enter a new coaching situation, the players may be unwilling to accept tight discipline, particularly if their recent teams have been substandard. You should expect to lose a certain amount of players who, because they are unused to your philosophy and unwilling to give your style of coaching a chance to succeed with them, refuse to accept your philosophy or techniques, including discipline. As you settle into your new situation, however, you normally will attract an increasing number of players into your program who think as you do, or who at least respect your efforts as being best for them.

You cannot win consistently with athletes who are neither self-disciplined nor willing to accept externally-imposed discipline.

FEAR

Fear is a double-edged sword. While fear of losing or failing to do one's best is a powerful motivator, athletes must be able to overcome fear in pressure situations in order to win consistently. As one coach has said, "Show me a team with a long losing streak, and I'll show you a team that has lost its fear of losing. It's not that they (the players) don't mind losing; it's just that they aren't *afraid* to lose."

Fear of Losing

Fear manifests itself in many ways. First, of course, there is *fear of losing*. While no one wants to lose, some athletes are more competitively oriented than others. Highly competitive athletes are often able to transform their fear into aggressiveness, which tends to enhance their performance in pressure situations. The coach quoted previously explained this point: "It's not superplays by superstar athletes that win or lose most games; it's ordinary plays executed in pressure situations by ordinary athletes." And since most players' performances tend to suffer to some extent in pressure situations, many coaches feel that more games are lost than won in pressure situations.

Success-oriented athletes—those who *expect* to win rather than merely *hope* to be victorious in competition—are generally more effective in pressure situations than athletes who either are unable to overcome their fear of losing, or else have grown so used to losing that winning is no longer a paramount objective for them.

In a recently televised basketball game, one of the announcers predicted early in the contest that "(Team A) is going to lose this game." Obviously shocked at this pronouncement, his partner on the telecast asked him what he was basing his prediction on. "Because," the first announcer replied, "(Team A) isn't playing to win. They're playing not to lose. You can't do that and win."

Team A lost the game. They managed to keep the score close throughout, but they lost. To win, you have to do what it takes to win, including overcoming your fear of losing. Anyone can lose; not everyone can overcome his/her fear of losing.

A later section of this chapter ("Using Threatening Situations,") deals with ways coaches prepare their players to deal with pressure situations.

Fear of Failure

A second type of fear affecting athletes is *fear of failure*. While fear or losing and fear of failure are synonymous in most respects, the latter also encompasses those players whose timidity or low threshold for embarrassment induces them to set goals so low that they never accomplish anything in athletes.

Fear of failure can be overcome if it is caught early enough in an athlete's career. Alexander Pope wrote, "As the twig is bent, the tree's inclined." Self-confidence is a learned trait; young athletes should be exposed to enough positive experiences early in their developmental stages to permit them to develop confidence in their ability to perform skills in competitive situations.

Fear of Rejection

A third fear is that of *rejection*, whether by teammates, the coach, family members, fans, or whomever the athlete is afraid of disappointing or letting down. Fear of rejection normally is a powerful, enduring motivator, one of the key ingredients (along with fear of losing and fear of failure) in the makeup of the self-motivated athlete.

Athletes normally want to live up to the expectations set for them by their parents, peers and coach. Peer pressure is a subtle, yet undeniably powerful, motivator, as is the positive relationship between players and coach.

The most common method of motivating players through their fear of rejection is to ignore the player in question, in the hope that the player will come to you when his sense of rejection is great enough. Such a ploy will not work, however, if the player does not in fact fear rejection by the coach.

Fear of the Coach

The most notorious condition involving players and fear is that of fear of the coach. The coach has at his command a variety of techniques such as punishment or threats for instilling fear into his players.

While fear of the coach may serve to motivate certain athletes, others are literally devastated emotionally by negative experiences with their coaches. Constant criticism, especially negative criticism, increases players' anxiety and reduces the enjoyment they derive from playing the game. And while there's more to competitive sports than mere enjoyment of playing the game, the fact remains that players operating in an environment of constant negativity are far more likely to quit their teams than players who do not live in constant fear of their coaches.

Fear of Injury or Pain

A type of fear commonly encountered, especially on lower levels of play, is that of *fear of injury or pain.* While fear of injury or pain is not a motivating force, its effects on affected athletes are usually powerful enough to negate the coach's finest motivational efforts. A would-be tackler in a junior high football game turns his back on an opposing ball carrier in order to avoid potentially painful contact, unaware that by such action he is increasing his chances of being injured on the play. There is no known antidote for this sort of malady, except perhaps switching to a type of sport (or to another position within a given sport) where injury and contact are less likely to occur.

AROUSAL

The term *arousal* refers to the amount of emotional involvement an athlete brings to competition. Some players are more easily aroused than others, and some players reach higher levels of arousal than others.

At first thought, one is tempted to conclude that the greater the level of arousal a coach can elicit from his/her players, the greater the team's chances for winning will be. As Robert Singer (1975, p. 54) has pointed out, however, while activities involving strength, endurance and/or speed are likely to be enhanced by increased arousal, the exact opposite is true regarding activities that involve finely tuned, highly coordinated movements (e.g., shooting a basketball, passing a football, or putting a golf ball).

USING THREATENING SITUATIONS

We coaches place a great deal of emphasis on *pride*. Our cheer-leaders boast that "We've got PRIDE on our SIDE!" and either we're glad that it's true, or else we wish it were so. A sense of pride—not to be confused with arrogance, conceit or haughtiness—can serve to trans-form a group of individuals into a closely knit team.

Pride consists of a sense of accomplishment associated with past achievements which affords an individual or team confidence in its ability to meet present and future challenges. Unfortunately, pride cannot be maintained at a constantly high level unless the team wins more often than occasionally. It takes an exceptionally gifted motivator to build pride overnight in a situation in which losing is accepted as a way of life.

Vince Lombardi (1973, p. 14) contended that winning and losing are both habits. A winning tradition is a situation in which winning is an expected outcome. The more a team wins, the prouder and more confident its members become of their ability to win. The more pride they feel, the harder they will fight to continue to win. The harder they fight to win, the more they will win, as positive expectations bring about increased efforts which in turn increase the likelihood of positive results.

The team with a winning tradition has something of value to protect: its ability to win. And, having experienced the thrill of victory, the players do not want to undergo the agony of defeat. It is precisely at this point where threatening situations come into play.

Definition

"Threatening situations" are those which serve to remind the competitors of what they stand to lose. In games, threatening situations are those situations in which the players, coaches and fans realize that the outcome of the game is on the line: for example, the bases loaded in the bottom of the ninth inning with two outs and the tying (or winning) run at bat. In practice sessions, threatening situations are artifically contrived conditions which simulate actual game conditions—or, more simply, they are situations created by the coach to teach players how to deal with pressure. Players who are taught to deal with pressure situations in practice should be able to deal with most threatening situations in games.

Setting Up Threatening Situations

To be effective, threatening situations must be competitive in the sense of accomplishing, or failing to accomplish, an objective. This in turn can mean either that two or more players are set against each other, or that an individual is placed in a situation in which the success or failure of his/her own efforts can spell victory or defeat for the team (e.g., shooting free throws or kicking field goals under simulated game conditions). Every coach should, through study of drills books, attending coaching clinics or talking with other coaches, search for competitive drills that can be used to prepare his/her players to function normally under the abnormal stress of threatening situations. Every such drill should include three clearly defined components: objective, process and outcome.

The *objective* of the drill(s) should be explained clearly enough that every player understands his/her own role in the process. The *process*—for example, working on a two-minute "hurry-up" offense in football for situations in which a team is behind in the fourth quarter with time running out—should be as specific as possible in such details as time limits and score. The *outcome* should provide immediate, easily recognizable feedback concerning success or failure.

Teaching Players to Concentrate

Distressed by his players' inability to make free throws in games, an Oregon high school boys' basketball coach came up with the somewhat dubious idea of having his players take off an article of clothing every time they missed a free throw in practice after school one day. During the practice, however, three members of the girls' drill team wandered into the gym to find one player in his undershorts and two other boys wearing nothing but their shoes and socks.

While most coaches would not take such a senseless, foolhardy risk as letting players practice in the nude, the fact remains that players must learn to concentrate under adverse conditions and the presence of distractions. One commonly encountered method used to prepare players during preseason practice is to have periodic scrimmages open to the public. Another popular technique involves scrimmaging with background music turned up to full volume in order to simulate crowd noise. (Care should be taken not to use music that the players like too much; after all, the purpose of the technique is to use noise to distract the players, not to entertain them.)

The threat of punishment can provide powerful inducement for players to take their time while practicing complex motor skills such as shooting a basketball or hitting a baseball; it cannot, however, improve skills or guarantee improved concentration. All the threats in the world are not going to make it any easier for a batter to hit a curve ball, since the complex neuromuscular interactions involved may be beyond the athlete's skills regardless of the level of his concentration.

CHAPTER 12

Motivation in Practice and in Games

HOW TO KEEP PRACTICE FROM BECOMING A DRUDGERY

Including pre-season practice, in-season practice and play, and post-season practice and play, a high school sport season normally involves three months or more of daily practice—and collegiate and professional seasons may last longer than half of the year. Many coaches find it difficult to maintain player enthusiasm for practice as the season wears on and takes its toll both mentally and physically. Some of those coaches try to alleviate the tedium of daily practice through use of any or all of the following four principles and techniques:

1. *Limit the number of players on your squad to those who can either contribute to the team's success or gain from the experience in ways that will help the team in the future.* If players are going to stand around at practice, there's no real logic in having fifteen varsity players on your basketball team just because you have fifteen uniforms avail-

able. The extra players are likely to require busy work to keep them from loafing or playing around while you're working with other players, and they (or their parents) may resent the lack of playing time they receive.

Jerry Tarkanian of the University of Nevada at Las Vegas prefers to have no more than eight superior athletes on his basketball teams at one time, and for the reasons cited previously. Still, he stresses, those eight athletes must be thoroughbreds if his "Hardway Eight" style of play is to be successful.

2. *Organize your practices in such a manner as to keep everyone busy.* One way to keep your athletes busy at practice is to organize the bulk of your practice sessions into a series of drill segments of only a few minutes' duration each. Another technique involves mixing up your drills and conditioning activities rather than grouping them together near the beginning or end of practice. A third method is to make as many of your drills competitive as possible, since players normally enjoy competing against each other, whether individually or in teams.

3. *Give your players a day off from practice every now and then. Or take time out from regular practice periodically to indulge in "fun" activities which may or may not be directly related to your sport.* When a team is doing poorly, the season seems a thousand years long. When a team is doing well, tension increases as playoffs near. In either case, taking a day off from time to time can give your team a badly needed mental lift.

In like manner, a gloomy practice atmosphere can be lightened considerably by taking time out for nonessential "play." (The play need not be nonessential; it can be functional as well, as in practicing pickoff moves vs. base stealing in baseball, or playing "tag" while practicing weak hand dribbling in basketball.) Bear Bryant once took time out from practice to hold a left-footed kicking contest to ease his players' tensions before an important game. (Bryant, 1974, pp. 115–16.)

4. *Divert players' attention from the drudgery of practice. Reward perfect attendance and superior effort at practice.* Track Coach Rod O'Donnell (1975, p. 24) challenges his cross-country runners to run a given amount of distance in a specified time period. If the athlete achieves the required distance in the time allotted, he is rewarded with a small trophy or a special patch he can wear on his jacket. Football coach John Staples (1978, p. 16) has suggested giving an "Iron Man"

plaque to every player who attends every practice, team meeting, and game throughout the season. The promise of rewards bring a positive atmosphere to practices that might otherwise be considered a drudgery.

HANDLING PLAYERS WHO DON'T LIKE TO PRACTICE

In discussing the problem of handling players who don't like to practice, the vast majority of veteran coaches I talked with favored a hard-line approach. Typical of the comments I collected are the thoughts of one football coach with sixteen years of coaching experience.

> I just can't understand a kid like that, one who doesn't like the sport he's playing enough to go hard at practice. I don't like having kids like that on my team.
>
> If a boy has some kind of legitimate excuse, or some physical problem that keeps him on the sideline, that's one thing—but a kid who goofs off at practice, clowns around while the others are trying to work, comes to practice late a lot of the time or skips practices, or loses his uniform or equipment—well, those are headaches I don't really need.
>
> I don't care if a kid is the best looking athlete since Hercules, I'll put his butt on the bench in a second if he's a starter and he thinks he's gonna disrupt my practice and make my life miserable! And if he doesn't like bench duty, he can always work his way back onto the starting lineup by improving his practice performances.

The greatest problem associated with hard-line approaches is that you stand to lose a lot of potentially fine athletes that way. And while coaches such as the one previously quoted contend that the risk of losing an athlete is more to be desired than the risk of having a team torn apart by the presence of a double standard of practice behavior, other, more positive approaches exist which may bring about needed changes in practice behavior without risking undesirable decisions by the coach or athlete regarding playing time or remaining on the team.

1. *Consider the player and the situation.* Are you sure the player in question is actually loafing when he stands around or makes lackadaisical mistakes in scrimmaging? He may not fully understand the responsibilities of his position. If an offensive tackle is confused about

his blocking assignment on a given play, for example, he is likely to either block the wrong person, or fail to block anyone at all. His confusion may force him from an active to a reactive role, in which case his effectiveness probably will be sharply reduced until his assignment is made perfectly clear to him.

I suggest an "ABCDEF" approach to teaching skills and patterns as the answer to problems such as the one previously cited:

"Always Be Careful to Demonstrate and Explain Fully."

A second consideration concerning the player in question is that communication is the key to understanding, whether on a personal or professional level. The coach who berates or punishes a player for problems of the sort described previously without first taking the athlete aside to discuss the problem is asking for trouble. Factors the coach may be unaware of may be at work, such as personal problems, illness or minor injuries. Or, if the coach is in his/her first year of coaching at the school, the previous coach may have had a relaxed attitude toward attendance and behavior at practice.

Of course, the player may in fact be at fault, but it's best to attempt to find out what the problem is before attempting to deal with it.

At any rate, there are two *don'ts* that the coach should consider regarding players who exhibit undesirable practice habits or attitudes: *don't* ignore such behavior; and *don't* wait for the situation to worsen before dealing with it.

2. *Consider the rest of your team: do your other players have similar attitudes?* If more than one or two of your players are guilty more often than occasionally, perhaps the real culprit is your situation rather than your players. In a normal situation, most of your players will enjoy, and look forward to, your practices, regardless of how rigorous those practices are, because they love the sport. And if your players don't love your sport—well, you have a major rebuilding task ahead of you in terms of changing attitudes.

3. *Peer disapproval is always a powerful motivator.* If you're having trouble with one of your players at practice, you might try having one or more other players get on that player's case, urging the player to work harder and complaining loudly when the player begins to slack off—if, that is, those players agree with your analysis that the player in question should be working harder.

In order to ensure that the player's teammates are aroused by lackadaisical performances at practice, some coaches punish not only the offender, but his/her teammates as well. And in a bizarre variation of this ploy, a few coaches punish, not the offender, but the rest of the team.[1]

4. *Study your practice schedule objectively and at length. Is it too demanding? Too dull? Too long?* If your answer to any or all of these factors is *yes*, you are referred to the previous section, "How To Keep Practices From Becoming A Drudgery."

5. *Use self-motivating drills to ensure that players work hard in practice.* I've grown increasingly interested in recent years in finding drills that automatically motivate players to work hard. Such drills have two elements in common: they are competitive, and they possess built-in penalties for failure to perform properly.[2]

You don't have to spend time motivating your players to work to maximum in practice if you can come up with drills that do the motivating for you. It's an interesting idea, one worthy of consideration, particularly if you sometimes have trouble motivating certain players in practice without resorting to prolonged periods of fun and games.

GUIDELINES FOR PRE-GAME, HALFTIME AND POST-GAME TALKS

Pre-Game and Halftime Motivation

Since halftime talks usually must be devoted primarily to strategy and tactical adjustments, coaches normally deliver their motivational talks before games. These pre-game and halftime talks may be either of two types, strategic (explaining the Xs and Os of the game plan to the players) or motivational (emotional appeals).

---

[1]Whether such tactics are desirable, or even ethical, is a question each coach must decide for himself/herself. Still, such ploys exist, and a book purporting to deal with coaching problems must address itself to the broadest possible range of solutions that have been attempted.

[2]In order to be most effective, penalties should be free from the coach's subjective evaluation of whether or not a player is hustling.

The first point to consider regarding motivational talks is that they aren't always necessary. Sometimes it's better to be businesslike in your pre-game remarks to the team.[3]

A second point concerning motivational talks is that they require advance planning and preparation. Successful motivational talks seldom are entirely spontaneous or impromptu. Best advice here is to: know what you want to say before you say it; say it; then stop. Doing more (or less) than this will defeat your purpose.

Third: as has been explained previously, highly emotional motivational appeals may adversely affect the performance of high-strung athletes, or athletes who must execute such complex, finely coordinated motor skills as shooting a basketball, hitting a baseball, swinging a golf club correctly, or passing a football accurately.

Fourth: be honest with your players. Perhaps it's just a pet peeve of mine, but I cannot accept the idea of telling my players in my pre-game pep talk that we're going to whip tonight's opponent even though they've won 87 straight games, our own losing streak stands at 23 games and if odds were being offered on the game we'd be 2,000,000-to-1 underdogs. To me, at least, a lie is a lie is a lie, whether it's a little white lie or a Watergate coverup.

If I don't think we can beat a given opponent even with our best effort, I won't lie to my players. Instead, I'll direct their attention away from winning and losing by telling them precisely what I expect each person to accomplish in the game in terms of individual and team assignments and effort. I'll describe the opponents' style of play, their strengths and weaknesses (if any), and tell the players how we can best take advantage of our strengths and/or their weaknesses. I'll try to motivate them toward giving their best effort throughout the game mentally and physically; but I won't lie and tell them that their best effort is going to produce a victory. Instead, I won't mention winning or losing at all.

Against a vastly superior opponent, then, a coach may find it worthwhile to stress goals other than winning or losing—which may not be such a bad idea against *any* opponent, either. Young people have a knack for knowing when their elders are lying to them—and it's

---

[3]This is not to say that you should not try to motivate your players for every contest, but rather to suggest that you should vary your techniques from game to game. You can't "Win One For The Gipper" every game.

just not worth the risk of having my players lose faith in me, for me to take a chance on lying to them.

In my first year of coaching at Toombs Central High School, I watched a very good Patterson (Ga.) Eagles team play in the state basketball tournament. I came away from the game worried about our chances against them next year. Their lineup was solid, well-balanced, deep, and tall.

Next season, I went to considerable lengths to warn my team that they'd better be ready when Patterson came to town. I was quite concerned about our chances in the game.

We led at halftime, 42–3.

And my team never again believed me that year whenever I tried to tell them how tough our next opponent was going to be.

Another advantage in being honest with the players is that they're likely to see through any false front you try to put up, anyway. For example, I don't think it's necessary or proper to maintain an air of confidence throughout every game day lest the players sense that you're not sure of victory. I'm a very nervous type of person, so instead of trying to hide my nervousness—which I couldn't do if I tried—I just try to control it by not fainting or throwing up in the players' presence. When players ask me if I'm nervous, I say, "Sure, I am." If they ask why, I'll either reply jokingly, "If you had to coach *you*, wouldn't you be nervous?," or else I'll tell them that I'm just a nervous person. So I haven't told them anything new.

A coach has told me that he thinks his body language on game day—his gestures, mannerisms, demeanor, etc.—transmit a sense of victory or defeat to the players. I'd substitute the words *confidence* or *nervousness* for victory and defeat. And although the majority of coaches probably prefer to be seen as confident, I don't. Neither does Head Basketball Coach Jerry Tarkanian of the University of Nevada at Las Vegas. Coach Tarkanian is a nervous person who has been known to chew on towels during games. (He also has won more than 84 percent of his games as a college basketball coach over a twenty-year coaching career.) He feels that, because an extremely fine line exists between confidence and overconfidence, he'd rather not portray confidence personified in the final hours before a game. Coach Tarkanian would rather create an atmosphere of tension that builds and builds as game time nears. He wants his players wound up tight as a spring by game time, ready to explode into action on the court.

Rather than reintroduce material from Chapter 5 at this point, I'll refer the reader to pp. 48–51 for a fuller description of Coach Tarkanian's motivational techniques. Still, we should note that, rather than attempting to conceal or deny his nervousness, Coach Tarkanian *uses* that nervousness as part of his motivational strategy. He feels that it's preferable to trying to assume a game-day personality that is alien to his true nature.

And I do *not* mean to infer here that exuding confidence is not a desirable goal for the coach on game day, or that coaches who display confidence on game day are necessarily lying to their players. Rather, I simply contend that an alternative viewpoint exists, and if, like me, you're a nervous type of person, you might consider the notion of using that tension to motivate your players rather than trying to conceal it.

Leaving aside personality and idiosyncracies of human nature for a moment,[4] in terms of strategy alone it's probably desirable for the coach to act as a foil to his/her players' expectations by taking an opposite viewpoint from theirs concerning the upcoming game. Thus, if the players are confident (as when they are facing an easy opponent), the coach should be tense and worried, in order to remind the players that, while confidence alone does not win games, overconfidence can lead to losing games. On the other hand, if the players are uptight and nervous (as when they are playing an opponent of equal or superior strength), the coach should assume an air of confidence, as if he/she *knows* that the team will give its best effort, and that that effort will result in victory.

Although you should talk to other coaches about motivational approaches and tactics they've used, you should remember, too, that motivational talks sometimes backfire. Paul "Bear" Bryant (1974) has told the story of his decision to wake up his players and call a 2:00 a.m. team meeting the night before a game. At the meeting, Bear told his groggy players the Biblical parable of the mustard seed and sent them back to bed.

A few days later, after Alabama had clobbered its latest opponent, Coach Darrell Royal of the University of Texas called Bear. Royal explained that he was worried about an upcoming game, and asked if Bear had any ideas about how Royal might motivate his team. Natur-

---

[4]If, indeed, personality and human nature can ever be left aside when it comes to discussing motivation.

ally, Bear told Royal about the 2:00 a.m. meeting and the mustard seed story, and how he felt it had contributed to the Tide victory. Royal thanked Bear and hung up shortly thereafter.

Emulating Bear's tactics to the letter, Royal roused his Longhorns at two o'clock in the morning, related to them the story of the mustard seed, and dismissed them to return to their beds. Next day, Royal's Texas Longhorns absorbed the worst defeat to that point in Coach Royal's career.

So much for mustard seeds and pre-dawn team meetings.

Post-Game Talks

Concerning post-game talks, two considerations arise: first, the coach should talk to the players in the dressing room after every game, regardless of whether the team won or lost and regardless of the margin of victory or defeat. Second, the period immediately following a defeat is a poor time to dress down players verbally for poor performances, since the coach's emotions may cause him/her to say things that will be regretted later. Too, the coach should remember that undue negativism at this stage may have an adverse effect on the team's performance next game.

The coach's post-game comments to the players should involve a rational, objective analysis of individual and team performances. One way to avoid emotionalism is to wait until after you've had time to study the game stats carefully before commenting at length on individual performances. From my own experience in keeping football statistics, I've come away from games convinced that a certain defensive player had done a fine job, only to find after compiling the stats that he'd made two or three tackles during the opponents' first possession, then contributed nothing further until late in the fourth quarter when the outcome was decided and the opponents had their scrubs on the field. Statistics can be deceiving, but the coach's first impressions immediately following a contest may be even farther from the truth.

GAME BEHAVIOR

The first point to be made concerning a coach's game behavior is that there are no immutable, hard-and-fast rules for coaching conduct or behavior, beyond reasonable moral and ethical considerations. Can a coach justify attempting to cheat (e.g., telling a player to fake an injury to gain an extra time out, or attempting to switch players at the free throw line to get a better shooter on the line instead of the player who was fouled)? Is a coach justified in telling a player to "get" an opponent? The answer, of course, is *no* to both questions. No circumstances are sufficient to condone cheating or dirty playing. The coach who permits or encourages his/her players to cheat or play dirty will be hard put to justify his existence as an educator.

Beyond this, probably the best guideline to game behavior for coaches is, *Be yourself.* That's what you do best, anyway. It's the way your players relate to you already. And in trying to put on a different game face you may find yourself unable to relate normally to your players.

One aspect of game behavior many coaches—myself included—need to work on is that of becoming so emotionally involved in games that we lose sight of our game plan. We are making a grave mistake when we permit our emotions to build to the point of blinding us to strategy and tactics that could be used to help our teams to function better in games. We may prefer to think that we're helping our players to maintain a high degree of intensity in their performances, but we're not. All we're doing is wasting time that could be put to better use studying situations arising within the flow of the game.

The very best motivators in coaching seldom rage and storm along the sidelines throughout games.[5] They don't need to. They know that it's also possible to get points across to their players quietly from time to time. And they know when to display emotion from the sidelines.

The Dallas Cowboys' head coach, Tom Landry, feels that players respond more positively to the image of a calm, confident head coach than to any emotions the coach might display on the sidelines.

Still, many coaches feel that displaying emotions and exuding confidence are not mutually exclusive acts. They contend that the good coach will use either or both to motivate his/her team as the situation dictates. The University of Maryland's flamboyant head basketball coach, Charles G. "Lefty" Driesell, is a master at the art of

---

[5]The most notable exception to this "rule" is ex-Head Football Coach Woody Hayes of Ohio State University, who was also one of the finest coaches in the history of college football.

motivating UM fans at Cole Fieldhouse to get behind the Terps. Technically, of course, Lefty's act (standing up, turning to face the crowd and waving his arms wildly in the air) is illegal under collegiate and high school basketball rules and deserves a two-shot technical foul call against him—but referees don't always see Lefty doing his thing. And even if the referees called the technicals, Lefty probably would consider them a small price to pay for getting twelve thousand screaming Terp fans into the act at Maryland's home basketball games.

PART FOUR

SITUATIONAL
MOTIVATION

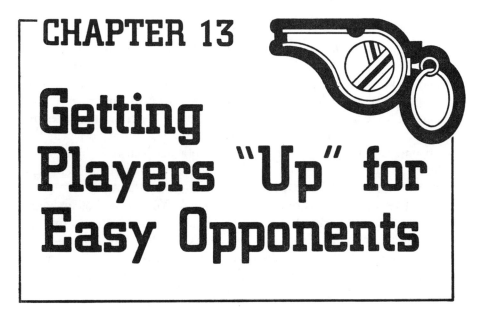

CHAPTER 13

Getting Players "Up" for Easy Opponents

Normally, you shouldn't have a difficult time motivating your players for games with traditional rivals or teams of strength equal to your own. You may be able to use the challenge of beating a superior opponent to prepare your team to face stronger teams. But what do you do to get your players up for games against weak opponents? How do you deal with the possibility of your players' taking an upcoming game for granted because you're expected to win easily? Many coaches rate games against weaker opponents as being among the most difficult motivational situations they face.

DEALING WITH OVERCONFIDENCE

When your team is heavily favored, your players may decide that all they have to do is show up for the game, and the opponents will cower in fear and trembling at the sight of your uniforms. As a coach, you know better than that, of course—you know, for example, that the opposing coach has done everything in his power to convince his players that they can beat you if they work hard enough. You know, too, that the coach may be right if your own players don't take the game seriously. Still, convincing your players that they're in for the fight of their lives may be a tall order.

If you play a team more than once in a single season, your players may not be aware of the extent of the opponents' weakness before you play them the first time. It would be a serious mistake for you to emphasize that weakness in discussing the upcoming game with your players, except in terms of describing how to plan to attack them. Then, in the game, some coaches would suggest that you beat the opponents convincingly the first time—not necessarily by a score of 96–7, or anything like that, but badly enough to convince them that they're not going to beat you next time you play them.

Every game starts out even. Zero-zero. You hope that, at some time or another during the game, your players will be able to build a lead sufficient to convince the opponents that they are beaten—and the sooner the better, as far as you're concerned. If you put them away early and then let them come back on you, two undesirable situations may arise: first (and worst), the opponents may regain enough composure, confidence and intensity to come back and beat you even after you put your starters back in; and second, even if you manage to beat them, they may not be convinced that they can't beat you next time.

It wasn't until my eighth year of basketball coaching that I learned to close the door on opponents when I had them put away. I was lucky enough to survive the experience without losing, but not because of any brilliance on my part.

We were playing at home, and leading by fifteen points midway through the third quarter when I decided that, since we already had the game won, I'd bench my regulars and give my second- and third-stringers some playing time before the home crowd. When the opponents began to come back on us a short time later, I didn't want to admit that I'd made a mistake, so I kept my key players on the bench as long as possible. Our lead dwindled to nine points, then five, then two, and by the time I got my starters back onto the court we were down three points with a minute left in the game.

We managed to come up with a steal and a rebound of a shot they shouldn't have taken, and threw in two desperation shots to win by one point, despite my best efforts to lose the game. I was fond enough of winning to appreciate my good fortune and to vow that I'd never let it happen again the way it did that night. And I haven't.

STRESSING INDIVIDUAL GOALS

The easiest way to keep your players hungry when they know that your next opponent is a pushover is to stress individual goals. Don't try to get your team up for the game; instead, talk to the players individually prior to the game and explain carefully how outstanding performances can improve their individual statistics.

I once listened as a football coach used this technique to motivate certain players against a weaker team.

"John," the coach said, addressing one of his starting defensive tackles, "you didn't have but four tackles last week. Tonight's going to be 'stat-fattening night' for you."

"Let's see." (The coach paused to check the stat sheets.) "You're averaging a little more than seven tackles a game. If you get sixteen tackles tonight, John, you'll raise your average to ten tackles a game. And you'd better believe that those double-figure stats impress the college coaches!"

Then the coach changed his approach slightly. "Now, I'm going to do you a favor, John, and let you play as long as it takes for you to get those sixteen tackles. All I ask in return is that you give me the kind of effort tonight that it takes to give you a shot at getting those sixteen tackles."

Another change. "You know, Harold (John's back-up at defensive tackle) would dearly love to fatten *his* stats tonight, too, John, but I think you'd like to reach that ten-tackles average even more. And I'm going to give *you* first chance at it. I hope you plan to take advantage of it."

"I will, Coach," the player said. (He did, too: his final stats showed fourteen tackles, four assists and a fumble recovery. No letdown there.)

Of course, the coach talked to Harold, too. "John needs a good game tonight, Harold—but so do you. You could use a ten-tackle game tonight, couldn't you?" (The coach paused for Harold to nod his agreement.) Then the coach pointed out that, because John wanted so badly to play well in that particular game, Harold must be ready to take full advantage of the opponents' weakness this week during *his* playing time if he hoped to improve his own statistics.

Thus, the coach was setting the stage for (a) a superior effort by his first-string defensive tackle, and (b) a superior effort by the second-string defensive tackle in the event that (a) did not take place.

The coach parceled out similar assignments to his assistant coaches after briefing them on the approach he wanted them to take. In one case, an assistant used a slightly different approach from the one used by the head coach.

To Marcus, a starting tight end, he said, "You haven't had a good practice all week. You've been dragging around, and frankly, I don't think you want to play tonight. I hope you prove me wrong, Marcus—but if you don't, you'll have plenty of time on the bench to think about it. I'll be glad to let Rusty (a reserve defensive back) take your place. I think Rusty's ready for a good game if you're not."

Then the assistant coach talked to Rusty. "Are you ready?," he asked. The boy said that he was.

"I hope so," the coach said. "Because we're going to blow this team off the field. *Somebody's* going to have a great game at tight end for us tonight, and from the way you and Marcus have been practicing lately, I think it'll be *you* if you're ready for it tonight!"

Beating *any* opponent can be challenging; all of us know that. But you can use individual goals to motivate your players to take full advantage of opponents' weaknesses when they might otherwise simply go through the motions of playing because they expect to win anyway, regardless of how ineffectually they play.

THE VALUE OF A HIGH-POWERED OFFENSE

When you have a high-powered offensive attack, it's easy to motivate your players. When players expect to score a lot of points, whether individually or as a team, they're going to work hard on offense and defense. In 1971–72, the Hobbs (N. M.) High School boys' basketball team averaged 115.7 ppg. Houston Wheatley High of Houston, Texas, scored a whopping 4,567 points, or 108.7 ppg., in compiling a 41–4 won-lost record during their 1972–73 season. (Both teams had other 100+ season averages during the '70s.) It's a good bet that the coaches of those teams didn't have two minutes' worth of trouble per season in motivating their players to go after the ball on defense, or to take advantage of scoring opportunities on offense.

Why? Because high scoring, or achieving other stellar individual and team statistics, is a tremendous motivating factor in players' performances. A halfback who averages 175 yards rushing per game over the first five games of a season is likely to be highly motivated to perform well in his sixth game, no matter who the opponent is. A basketball player with a 27-ppg. average knows that he/she must score at least 27 points in the next game in order to maintain that average.

This is not meant to imply that the halfback will perform as if his only goal is to reach 175 yards rushing; rather, he is more likely to enter the next contest wanting to do everything he can to get as many yards as possible. And if he is a truly outstanding performer, his teammates will share in the pride of his accomplishments, often to the extent of improving their own performances as well.

LETTING THE BIG DOG RUN

In 1979–80, the University of Georgia's football team had a 6–5 record. Not bad, but certainly nothing to write home about. The next year, freshman sensation Herschel Walker was the only significant addition to the squad, but his incredible performances (which included over 1,750 yards rushing in twelve games, ten scoring runs from scrimmage of 45 yards or more, 18 touchdowns and placing third in the 1980–81 Heisman trophy ballotting) led Georgia to a 12–0 season and a national championship.

Walker's performances clearly influenced Georgia's offensive linemen: they quickly learned that all they had to do was open half a hole in the offensive line for Herschel to run through, since he was likely to break any arm tackle by a defensive lineman or linebacker who was only partially blocked out of the play. Walker's incredible ability to break arm tackles in the line and then outrun defenders in the secondary made his offensive linemen appear better than they were; they, in turn, were eager to open holes for Herschel to run through, knowing that he would take full advantage of even the partial openings they created in the line.

It was a coach's dream come true for Head Coach Vince Dooley: Walker's performances consistently motivated his teammates in ways that Coach Dooley himself could never have achieved, and lifted the entire team to levels of performance they would never have been motivated to strive for otherwise (as witness the previous year's 6–5 record).

Of course, Vince Dooley didn't invent this technique; he merely used it to the fullest. The University of Southern California has used a succession of outstanding backs to demoralize opponents and motivate USC players to peak performances consistently.

SHOCK TREATMENT: THE USE OF MOTIVATIONAL GIMMICKS

Coaches have, on occasion, used gimmicks or shock techniques to stir their players out of complacency or lethargy, or to inspire them to performances which would normally be considered beyond the range of their ability.

If you're considering the possibility of using stunts to shock your players, you might consider the following guidelines:

1. *Save your stunts for special occasions.* Don't try to shock your players every game. Once or twice a season is plenty: more than that, and your stunts will lose their shock values. The players will still be interested, of course, but they may not be aroused to action. The value and appeal of shocking motivational gimmicks lie, not in their absurdity, but in their *unexpected* absurdity.

2. *Don't overdo your presentation.* Let the nature of the stunt speak for itself. Don't explain to the players what your stunt is supposed to mean; they'll know without your telling them. The easiest way to reduce the impact of your gimmicks is to discuss them with players after you've performed them.

3. *Look for opportunities to improvise gimmicks.* While your gimmicks normally should be planned and rehearsed before they are performed, you may find opportunities arising spontaneously or accidentally that you can take advantage of.

When Paul "Bear" Bryant was coaching at the University of

Kentucky, for example, he and his team arrived at the stadium for a road game with the University of Cincinnati only to find that, due to the difference in time zones, he'd misread the schedule and brought his players to the stadium an hour earlier than he was supposed to arrive. Rather than admit his mistake, Bear had his team suit up and go through their pre-game warmups an hour early in the empty stadium. When they finished their warm-up exercises and preparations, Bryant sent his squad back to the dressing room. For the next hour, Bear paced back and forth in front of the players without speaking.

The players, not knowing that Coach Bryant had made a mistake, quite naturally assumed that something important was happening—as indeed it was, an hour later when Bear unleashed his now fired-up squad on Cincinnati with one of the briefest pep talks in history: "Let's go."

Kentucky won easily, 27–7, over a favored Cincinnati team.

4. *Keep the number of people who know about your stunt to a minimum.* Assistant coaches should know about the stunt beforehand, of course, particularly if they're going to be involved in it, but they should be sworn to secrecy. Ohio State's Woody Hayes had his managers pre-cut his caps with razor blades so he could fling them off at practice, maybe stomp on them a couple of times, and then dramatically pick them up and rip them apart with his bare hands.

5. *Don't make players the butt of (or accomplices in) deceitful gimmicks or stunts intended to motivate them.* Players' feelings are not to be trifled with lightly. If they feel that they have been deceived, their confidence and respect for you will vanish quicker than you can say "Honest, kids, I didn't mean it!"

I was told of a coach who persuaded one of his starters—a player he trusted completely—to fake a knee injury in practice the day before an important game so he—the coach—could "heal" the player at a team meeting before they left for the game. The team lost, anyway.

Naturally, the player eventually told his teammates about the stunt. (He thought it was a good joke on them.) From that day on the coach's popularity (and his program as well) diminished until he finally left the school.

In another case, a coach's mother died. Although the coach wanted to use the occasion to motivate his players—an incredibly cold, heartless gesture—he was prevented from doing so by the fact that he'd already told his players that his mother had died to motivate them for a game the year before. Players' trust is not easily earned; the coach who has worked hard to earn his/her players' confidence, faith, respect and trust will not risk losing that bond for the possible motivation to be gained from a dishonest or deceitful gimmick played at their expense.

6. *Don't make absurd promises you don't intend (or aren't able) to keep.* On at least two occasions when Pepper Rodgers was coaching football at the University of Kansas, and later at UCLA, he promised his players that, if they beat an important rival, he'd lead the team out onto the field for the next game by doing a succession of back hand-springs. They won, and he did. But if, like me, you couldn't do a back handspring with the assistance of a trampoline, a safety harness and four strong spotters, you should not make any such promises. Your players are going to hold you to your promises if they win.

If, for example, you promise to run behind the bus on the trip home one mile for every point your team wins by—a fairly common ploy—what will you do when your team wins by thirty points? Will you qualify your conditions and hedge on your promise? Or will you try to run thirty miles?

The best solution is to think out your deal before you announce it to the players. You can promise to do the funky chicken with a cheer-leader at the next pep rally, or let the players take charge of part of the next practice session, with you and the assistants taking the players' places, or whatever comes to mind. But consider the possible outcome before you make your deal with the players. You'd better believe the players are going to hold you to the exact terms of your promise if they win. And if you renege on your word, they'll never again believe any promises you make.

7. *Don't waste your stunts on traditional rivalries, playoff games, or other contests you know your players are going to be "up" for anyway.* This is not to say, of course, that you shouldn't try to motivate your players for important games; still, you don't usually need gimmicks for games that your players are likely to be fired up for anyway. Shock treatments are normally reserved for either of two situations: those in which a team is flat or nonchalant about an upcoming game, or those in which the opponents are demonstrably more powerful and likely to walk away with an easy victory. A coach might bring out a new set of

uniforms for a particularly important encounter, but that's about the extent most coaches would want to involve themselves in surprise tactics where traditional or intersectional rivalries are concerned.

TRICK PLAYS

Coach Jim Trotter (1971, p. 18) has identified three types of trick plays: those that deceive through unusual formations or alignments; those that create confusion through rules misconceptions;[1] and plays that simulate one thing and do another.

Practicing and using trick plays serve utilitarian purposes such as putting points on the scoreboard and forcing opposing coaches who are aware of your tendency to use trick plays to waste their own practice time preparing to deal with your trick players. Beyond this, however, there are psychological ramifications to the use of trick plays which can serve to motivate your own team and deflate the morale of your opponents.

Players love to practice executing trick plays, and as long as the time spent working on such plays doesn't get out of hand, such activity is likely to provide welcome occasional relief from drudgery and grind in your daily practices. As Coach Trotter (1971) has pointed out, when you're winning, practicing trick plays keeps your players loose; and when you're losing it gives the players something to look forward to, it keeps their interest high, and it increases your chances of winning against superior opponents. And when your trick plays work in games, they give your players at least a momentary psychological advantage.

From your opponents' point of view, your unpredictability is likely to be unnerving. The ever-present possibility of your using trick plays can serve to keep opponents off balance and unsettled, even if their team possesses superior ability. They may be prepared to beat your strength with their strength, but when you succeed in overcoming their strength through the use of deception or trickery, they may become embarrassed or angry enough to lose their cool completely. When momentum subtly begins to shift in one team's favor as a result

---

[1]And, we might add, plays designed to take advantage of situations not adequately covered by present rules.

of a successful trick play, elements such as *fate* and *luck* enter the picture. And when luck becomes a factor in winning or losing, it's anybody's ball game.

As a close friend once told me, "I'd rather be lucky than skillful." I asked him why. He replied, "Skills may let you down, but you can always count on luck." The mental edge between winning and losing can be exceedingly thin at times. Trick plays can sometimes provide that edge.

CHAPTER 14

Forging Positive Attitudes and Relationships

PURSUING A WORK ETHIC

One of the first problems you are likely to encounter in building (or rebuilding) a successful program in your sport is that of forging positive attitudes and relationships. And while it is extremely unlikely that you will accomplish this goal overnight, you must begin immediately to reshape the attitudes of those around you in terms of the goals you intend to set for yourself, your players and your team.

A team's success is governed by many intangibles, the first of which is that *it has to mean something to your players to be on your team*. The more reasons your players have, or acquire, for participating in your sport, the easier your coaching will be. It is a grave mistake in judgment for any coach entering a new situation to assume that players have already discovered such meaning to their participation, particularly when their team has lost consistently in the past.

Finding Meaning and Purpose in Athletics

While working players hard in practice prepares them for the rigors of competition in games, it serves another, even more important function: helping players to find meaning and purpose in their athletic participation. Without exception, the players on your team who are most likely to grumble and complain about your coaching are those who do the least work. They grumble because they expect to reap a rich harvest of rewards from the fruits of others' labors, and because they neither fully understand nor appreciate the true value of their participation in athletics.

If you work your players hard enough in practice, they will have neither time nor inclination to grumble, complain, or cause trouble—and they will gain a sense of commitment to, and appreciation for, their participation in athletics. I've never known of any situation in sport in which players who regularly were required to work to the point of utter exhaustion felt compelled to complain about their lot[1], or objected to the hard work involved in their training.

In this regard, I like to use the example of mountain climbers, or mountaineers. It is difficult to conceive of a more dangerous or demanding physical activity than climbing mountains. Yet in many cases the mountaineers themselves cannot adequately explain their willingness to voluntarily undertake the incredible rigors and hardships involved in climbing a given mountain except in such simplistic terms as "because it's there," or "to get to the top." But if enjoying the view from a mountaintop were the only reward, they could, in many cases, get there faster, easier, and infinitely more safely, by hiring a helicopter pilot to transport them to the top.

If pressed further to explain their involvement, they are likely to reply in terms of the satisfaction of meeting challenges, overcoming difficulties, and exploring the limits of their endurance and ability. But are those answers adequate to explain why a person would voluntarily place himself in a situation in which a single misstep can mean death, merely for the sake of sport? Maybe. Still, it doesn't really matter whether we understand the meaning and purpose inherent in climbing mountains, or whether the mountaineer is able to put into words what inching up sheer mountain faces means to him. The important factor

---

[1]This statement includes professional as well as amateur sports. It was not entirely coincidental that major league baseball preceded professional football in free agentry and striking.

is that he accepts the challenges of mountain climbing, however he perceives them, as being in his best interests.

In like manner, your athletes will find that working hard to achieve meaningful goals brings its own rewards. Just as the mountaineer's ultimate goal—standing on top of the mountain and exulting in his achievement—is made possible only through the *process* of climbing the mountain, the athlete's ultimate goal—*winning*, in team sports—occurs through the process of playing the game. The greater the athlete's involvement in that process (i.e., the harder he extends himself toward the limits of his ability), the deeper his commitment to the sport, the team and winning, will be.

You have every right to expect your players to work to the limits of their ability to attain high levels of skills, both individually and as a team. Unfortunately, though, players who are used to losing are unlikely to understand—or, in some cases, to *accept*—the amount of hard work that goes into a winning effort. Your task, then, is obvious: to condition your players to accept hard work by teaching them why hard work is necessary.

It is not enough to tell your players that "If you work hard, we'll win." Players on consistently losing teams think they're working hard, too, even when their efforts are far below maximum. You must show them, by word and deed, that they are not working hard enough, or that their previous efforts have not been directed in proper channels.

Why Players Will/Will Not Work Hard for You

Let's assume that you've taken over a losing team. Several reasons exist why you can expect your players to work hard for you initially. A new season always brings new expectations for the players. Additionally, they are likely to respond favorably to your own positive expectations and approach. They may find your knowledge of the game superior to that of their former coach, or they may like the style of play you plan to use. They may believe that you actually *can* turn things around for the team. They may respond positively to your personality. Or they may be maturer than they were in the past, and thus more prepared to perform the skills you consider necessary.

There is, on the other hand, only one reason why they may not be willing to accept hard work. They may not be athletes; that is, their reasons for wanting to be on the team may have little or nothing to do with individual improvement or the pursuit of team goals. (For example, they may try out for the team because one or more of their friends are on the team, or because they—or their parents—like the idea of their wearing a team uniform.) You're likely to lose players with such shallow commitment when the hard work begins. But most of the real athletes, the ones you're counting on to turn things around in your program, won't quit on you. They may grumble occasionally about how hard you work them, but they'll probably go along with you just to see if you can produce what you say you will.

They may gripe and complain along the way, because they aren't used to the kind of effort you're demanding of them—but they'll stay with you. At least, most of them will. They may not believe you at first, but curiosity, if nothing else, will make them want to stick around for the finish.

COMMUNICATION: THE KEY TO MOTIVATION

There are coaches, and coaches. Some coaches are organized and businesslike in practice, and follow their practice schedules to the split-second; others prefer a more informal, spontaneous approach. Some coaches dislike being involved in their players' personal lives away from the playing field or gymnasium; others feel a sense of responsibility to their players that extends into their personal lives as well as their on-field or on-court performances. Without getting into the relative merits of the various approaches to the coaching task, it is important for the coach to understand the coach's role as he/she sees it, whether it be teacher, counselor, friend, parental figure, authority figure, cheerleader, or a combination of two or more of those roles.

The Coach and Communication

Most of us probably consider ourselves effective in the art of communicating with our players. Still, we would do well to remember that communication is more than talking. It also involves listening. And understanding. And believing. For many young people nowadays, listening itself is a lost art.

Consider the youngster's plight: virtually every adult in his/her life is either an authority figure or a talking head: teachers delivering lectures in class, preachers delivering sermons in church, the boss at work, parents; the numbing effect of television viewing, or rock/soul music played at 180 decibels; the prevalence of drugs in our society today, and their easy accessibility to teenagers. All of these and other factors serve to further isolate many young people for whom the act of growing up has already produced its own sense of alienation.

Enter the coach. If you want to be more than an authority figure or a talking head to your players, you're going to have to relate to them on their terms to a certain extent. And while this does not mean that you can or should try to turn the clock backward and become a teenager again yourself, it implies that there must be a willingness on the part of both player and coach to meet each other's needs.

Since coaching is your chosen profession—along with teaching, of course—you probably feel a deep need to build a successful program, preferably in your present situation. To do this, you need players who are committed to that goal.

Your players may not see it that way, of course. Because they are still growing up, their priorities are constantly changing. Athletics may be terribly important to them, but at this stage in their development it is not their life's work. They have other needs which must be met, and I think in too many cases we as coaches overlook the importance of those needs as perceived by the youngsters themselves.

A Personal Definition of Communication

To me, communication is what happens after my players realize that I am genuinely concerned about them as human beings as well as athletes. Young people are perceptive. And if they perceive us as being just another in a long succession of adults who have lied to them or tried to sell them a bill of goods, they'll tune us out in the blinking of an eye.

Communication as I perceive the term, then, consists of equal parts of *what* you say, *how* you say it, and *the environment you create* in which to say it. An exceedingly fine line exists between being yourself and being what the players want and need you to be. You must be yourself, since that's the only *you* you can portray honestly. Just as you may feel the need to understand your players, it is equally important for them to understand you. And since, for most youngsters, understanding *themselves* is at best a difficult and lengthy process, they are going to need all the help they can get in coming to the realization that you are an adult they can trust and depend on.

Four Steps Toward Communication

1. *You must have a clear plan of where you're going.* Without such a plan, you're unlikely to inspire confidence in youngsters who have no idea where *they're* going, whether in athletics or in life.

2. *You must be able to communicate that plan to your players in terms they understand.* The best plan in the world is useless if your players cannot execute it, or if they don't understand what you're trying to do.

3. *You must be able to let each player know exactly how he/she fits into your overall plans for the team.* The coach's efforts in this regard are integral in the process of molding individuals into a closely knit team. Players must be shown precisely how their contributions can help the team. Without that necessary step, their efforts are likely to be disoriented and misdirected.

4. *You must tell the players what you want often enough—and in enough different ways (e.g., slogans and posters on the dressing room walls, etc.)—that everyone understands what you're saying.* Tell them what you want them to believe, and why you believe it. Then tell them again. And again. And when or if you ever reach a point where you think they understand you, find another way to say the same thing, and tell them again.

"WHAT THE WORLD NEEDS NOW"—
THE LOVING RELATIONSHIP

It bears repeating that every coach has to use the approach that he/she is comfortable with. Away from games and practice, I go along with the words to a popular song from the '60s: "What the world needs now is love . . ." When an atmosphere of love and shared commitment exists among team members and the coaching staff, discipline is seldom a problem, nor is communication. Your players aren't always going to listen to you just because you love them—but at least they aren't going to tune you out because you *don't* love them.

As I said in the beginning of this section, there are coaches, and coaches. *You* may not believe in love as a factor in your team's success. Still, I'll guarantee you one thing: if you can teach your players to love each other, you'll never have serious motivation problems.

I have never consciously worked toward the goal of having my players like me. Oh, I suppose I prefer being liked to being disliked, but *liking* and *disliking* are surface feelings. What I'm after is something deeper: commitment. Outside of practice and games, virtually all of my coaching efforts are directed toward establishing an atmosphere of mutual respect and love. In such an environment, you have the potential to move mountains.

I was talking to a coach from another school one day when one of my players ran up to ask me a question. I answered her. As she turned to go, I called her. "Mary?"

She turned back to me. "Sir?"

"I love you, gal."

She smiled broadly, nodded, and trotted back to the group of girls she was with.

I turned back to the coach. He was staring at me in stunned silence, unable to believe his ears. That same year, though, we won the state championship in our first full year of girls' track. Mary won three events herself, including an all-classification state record in the 880.

I received two richly undeserved "State Coach Of The Year" awards. Undeserved, because all I did was surround myself with girls who would have literally run themselves to death before they'd let down their teammates or me.

The following year, with Mary graduated, we won the Region championship again in girls' track, but finished second in the State meet. Still, we finished 20–3 in basketball, with no one in the starting lineup taller than 5'5". In my vainer moments, I like to think that it was my coaching that brought about those successes. But it wasn't, not really, except in the sense that our team was a second family to the players. In some cases, they received more love from their teammates, my wife and me, than they received at home.

Player Conferences

Because communication involves (but is not confined to) talking, I use the first five minutes of practice every day to try to get across various points of my coaching philosophy to the team. On occasion, I'll single out certain players, praising them for their hard work or accomplishments, whether in athletics, the classroom, or in other phases of their lives. Although coaching is positive in the sense of teaching new skills, it is also negative in the sense of correcting mistakes. And since I'm always the first to criticize poor work or lackadaisical performances by my players, I try very hard to balance the ledger by singling them out individually for praise as often as their performances in practice and games warrant.

This task is particularly enjoyable for me when it involves players who are not accomplished athletes; sometimes it's the only praise these kids ever get. As I watch them react in surprise and embarrassment to this unexpected recognition, I'll say, "Get used to it; that's what it's like to be a superstar."

Along with team meetings, I think it's important to take time out as often as possible to talk with players individually—and not just the superior athletes, either—to transmit your personal concern for each and every player. In these conferences, I'll talk with them about any of a multitude of topics that need discussing: their athletic performances to date, the state of their health, personal problems, grades, how things are going at home, or whatever needs to be discussed or is important to them. And if I run out of things to say, I'll tell them that I love them and relate nice things their teammates or others in the school have said about them.

Basically, though, it doesn't matter what we talk about most of the time. The important factor is that I'm spending time with them individually, and taking the time to reaffirm their importance to me and to the team. I think it helps to remember what it was like to be an insecure teenager myself. *My* coach never did those kinds of things for me, and heaven knows I needed reassurance and a friendly pat on the back during those turbulent years.

Three final considerations: first, these are conferences, not lectures. If you intend to use them, you should try to maintain a casual, friendly tone throughout. Second, it doesn't hurt to let the player do some of the talking. Sometimes you'll find out about players' problems that you weren't aware of before. And you'd better believe that *your players' personal problems are your problems as well*, at least, when they begin to affect the quality of the player's performances. As Bear Bryant (1974, p. 14) has said, whatever the players consider important *is* important.

Third, address the player by his/her first name often in your conversations, particularly in compliments. If this technique is not overworked to the point of becoming meaninglessly repetitious, it can provide a useful way of getting the player's attention, and of underscoring the importance of what you're saying.

CHAPTER 15

Handling the Self-Motivated Athlete

UNDERSTANDING THE SELF-MOTIVATED ATHLETE

The self-motivated, or internally motivated, athlete is a relatively rare breed of individual. He/she is the type of player who seldom if ever complains about the length or difficulty of practices, and always gives his/her best efforts in practice and in games, regardless of other factors such as the importance of a given game or practice session, the score or the presence of minor physical ailments. Self-motivated athletes may or may not possess superior skills or ability, but since they normally are internally driven to give their best efforts without constant prodding by the coach, they are coachable and thus contribute greatly to team goals.

Because they do not require external motivation, however, such players tend to be overlooked by coaches, particularly when other, less highly motivated players command much of the coaches' attention in practices and in games. The prudent coach will find opportunities to recognize and reward the efforts of self-motivated athletes.

And because such athletes generally tend to be highly critical of their own performances, the prudent coach will take pains to offer constructive guidance and counseling on those occasions when the self-motivated athlete's performances do not reach his (the athlete's) expectations. It is a mistake to expect athletes to work out problems on their own; with self-motivated athletes, such an oversight can prove disastrous to the player and the team.

Self-motivated athletes are driven primarily by inner urges such as ego fulfillment, pride, fear or failure, an aggressive attitude, the challenge of competition, and/or many other complex and interacting factors. The coach—and, indeed, the athlete as well—may have little control over the personality traits that go into the making of a self-motivated athlete, since in most cases neither the coach nor the athlete was responsible for the environment in which the athlete's personality was formed during the earliest years of childhood.

John Turner (1979, p. 25) describes *self-discipline* as the beginning of internal motivation, extending one's performance through and beyond the pain barrier to persist even in the face of hardships, pressures and other counter influences. Possibly it is the ability to consistently play up to and through the pain barrier—and we're talking here about the ability to absorb pain and fatigue without suffering a drastic reduction in quality of performance—that separates the self-motivated athlete from other athletes. Turner listed desire and determination, drive and pride as the principal ingredients in internal motivation.

THE ROLE OF THE COACH

The coach's role in the motivation of athletes who are primarily self-motivated should be that of a positive reinforcer. If you study your athletes carefully to determine who needs to be prodded (pushing) and who needs to be led (pulling), you soon find that the self-motivated athlete normally requires little or no pushing *or* pulling in order to function effectively. The danger here is that, in our concern for other athletes who require constant external motivation, we may tend to overlook the needs and contributions of the self-motivated athlete.

Recognition

Self-motivated athletes should be singled out periodically for recognition among their peers concerning the quality of their efforts. This recognition, which serves as positive reinforcement for the athlete that he/she is contributing in the best way possible to the team's success, should be done both publicly and privately. Publicly, the coach should do all in his/her power to reward the efforts of internally motivated athletes, whether by bragging about the athlete to journalists and reporters, presenting awards to such players,[1] or otherwise publicly acknowledging such athletes' accomplishments and efforts.

Building a Bond of Understanding

Privately, the coach should take time to talk with the athletes on a personal basis periodically, not just to find out if they are having problems, but to thank them for their hard work and assure them that their efforts are contributing greatly to team goals.

For the most part, coaches are self-motivated individuals. And since a primary objective of any coach in any coaching situation is to surround himself with players who love his sport the way he does, it's natural for him to have a special affection for the highly motivated athletes he works with every day.

In theory, at least, you're supposed to treat all of your players alike, but it's just not possible where self-motivated athletes are concerned. As coaches, we're not supposed to play favorites—but I do, and you probably do, too. All of us do. We play the kids who will work as hard as they can to play the game the way we want them to. You may be a defense-oriented coach while I prefer offense (or vice versa), but *both* of us will favor those team members who believe that our way is best for them, and give their best efforts to play the game that way.

---

[1]Bear Bryant annually presented a "Jerry Duncan I Love To Practice" award to the Crimson Tide football player who best exemplified the qualities Duncan possessed. (Duncan, an Alabama player of little renown otherwise, became legendary at UA for the intensity of his efforts in practice.) Bear also used a "One Hundred Percent Club" with his teams, with membership qualifications based on effort rather than ability.

There's nothing wrong with that, either. St. Paul called it "the communion of like minds." I think, though, that we owe the team an honest expression of our feelings. There's nothing wrong with admitting to a bond of special affection for one player or group of players on the team, as long as (a) the affection is based on performance rather than personality, and (b) the rest of the players are not ignored or overlooked. Such an admission of high respect for a given player can, in fact, serve two purposes at once: first, the player in question receives powerful reinforcement concerning his/her status with the coach and the team; and other players, envious of such high regard, may increase the level of their own efforts.

Being self-motivated does not in itself mean that the athlete is either capable or desirous of functioning as a team leader. The coach should discuss this possibility with the athlete and provide opportunities for the player to assume leadership roles temporarily, but he should not try to force the athlete into the role of team leader against his will. People seldom function effectively when they are forced into unwanted leadership roles. Thus, it may be helpful to remember that self-motivation is *internal* motivation which the athlete may or may not be capable of externalizing.

On the other hand, the converse of the previous statement—that *effective team leaders are also self-motivated individuals (although they normally respond very well to coaching as well)* may prove helpful in identifying potential team leaders.

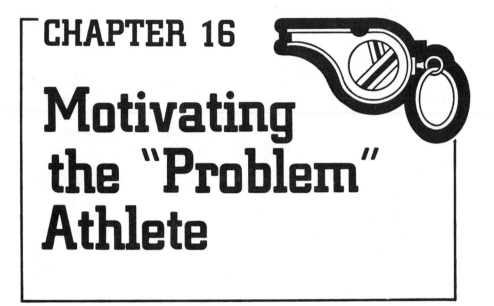

CHAPTER 16

Motivating the "Problem" Athlete

In terms of motivation, there are three types of athletes: self-motivated athletes, athletes who respond positively to external motivation such as that provided by the coach, and athletes who are not self-motivated and seldom respond to external motivation. "Problem athletes" are those who fall into the latter category.

All athletes have problems; "problem athletes" are those who, for whatever reason, either permit personal problems to affect their athletic performances, or else by their behavior create problems which adversely affect their own performances, and possibly the team's, as well.

PERSONAL PROBLEMS

Some coaches don't want to become involved in their players' personal lives. Still, sometimes it is difficult to avoid involvement: when personal problems affect your players' performances, you're already involved. You can't just tell a player to solve his own problems; he would gladly do so if he could. And those problems aren't going to disappear just because you want them to.

Ideally, players should leave their personal problems outside the gymnasium or away from the practice field. Realistically, though, problems are like emotions, in the sense that ability to control them depends upon their immediacy and severity.

If the coach is either unwilling or unable to work with players in solving their problems, he/she should at least be willing to steer the athlete toward others in the community who could conceivably help in dealing with the problem: the school counselor or counseling service; the athlete's minister or family physician; the community's family services center or health department; drug counselors; or whoever might be willing or able to help out.

BEHAVIORAL PROBLEMS

In their excellent book *Psychology Of Coaching*, Dr. Thomas Tutko and Jack Richards (1971) categorized problem athletes as follows: athletes who resist coaching; con men; hyper-anxious or psyched-out athletes; success-phobic athletes (athletes who fear winning); malingerers (athletes who fake or exaggerate injuries to get out of practice); withdrawn or suspicious athletes; and depression-prone athletes. Although these problems qualify technically as personal problems, their presence may result in aberrant or antisocial behavior that can destroy team morale and completely nullify the coach's motivational efforts.

Athletes Who Resist Coaching

Perhaps the two most frustrating statements coaches hear from their players are "I quit," and "I can't do it that way."

Concerning the former, I simply refuse to accept the statement we hear so often in education that *whenever a student* (read: student-athlete) *fails*, the *teacher* (read: coach) *fails*. It reads nicely, and the concept of shared responsibility is a cornerstone of contemporary educational theory—but personally, I just can't buy it as a universal truth.

In too many cases, youngsters come to us with deeply ingrained negative attitudes that neither we nor the youngster has control over.[1] We will, of course, work with such youngsters on an individual basis, but I for one think it's a cheap shot to automatically blame the coach whenever a player quits, or when the coach is unable to resolve the player's problems.

"I can't." Every coach has heard this response from players more times than he/she wants to remember. With some players, "I can't" is a way of life, a shield against having to try new things. What it really means is, "I'd rather do it *my* way." Or maybe not do it at all.

Athletes may resist coaching for any number of reasons—for example, they (or their parents) may feel that they deserve more playing time than they're getting; they may mistrust or dislike the coach; they may dislike the style of play the coach has adopted for the team; or they may selfishly want to play the game in their own way, and with their own best interests in mind rather than those of the team.

Coaches should strive to earn their players' trust and confidence, and the key in this regard is keeping lines of communication open between the players and the coach. The best way to deal with problems is to attempt to talk them out with the athlete concerned. Ideally, both parties should be willing to discuss problems objectively and give as much as necessary for the sake of the team. In practice, however, neither the coach nor the player may be willing to bend—and in such cases it is the coach's will that must prevail in the final analysis. While there is nothing wrong with letting players participate in the decision-making process—in fact, it is a very *good* policy for coaches to adopt—still, enormous differences exist between participating in and taking over the decision-making process.

Players should *never* be permitted to decide for themselves when they are going to hustle and when they are going to slack off. Even in practice, the coach has both the right and the responsibility to expect *every* player to work hard: when a player slacks off, he or she is cheating every other player on the team who continues to play hard—and when the coach does not correct these situations as they arise, he/she is reinforcing the idea that working and playing hard are not always important. This in turn increases the likelihood that such behavior will

---

[1]Or else they're into the drug scene, with its built-in nightmares.

be repeated in the future by the present offender and by other team members as well.

If the coach does not consider it important for players to hustle or give a total effort 100 percent of the time, he/she should define as precisely as possible the times when players will not be expected to work or play hard. Otherwise, players are likely to decide for themselves in this regard—and their decisions to slack off will occur almost invariably in important situations when outcomes of games are in the balance.

Note: If the player's resistance to coaching takes the form of inattentiveness more often than occasionally, particularly when you're talking to the team or explaining a given skill, you might want to have the player's hearing checked. The player may not be aware that he/she has suffered a hearing loss—and even if the loss is marginal, it can serve to make the player seem inattentive and unconcerned at times.

I have a congenital hearing problem myself, and I often find myself letting things slip by unheard rather than go through the embarrassing ordeal of having to ask the speaker four or five times what he/she said.

Con Men

Every coach sets standards of expected behavior for his/her players. These standards, arbitrarily selected, may be as important as rules governing drug abuse, or as apparently unimportant (to the players, at least) as the length of a boy's hair. As long as the rules are fully understood by the players, fairly administered by the coach and not too far off the wall in terms of arbitrariness, most players will make an honest effort to operate within the rules most of the time.

Occasionally, however, coaches encounter players who seem to take delight in testing the limits of the coach's commitment to the standards he/she has set. These are the "con men," or players who, for whatever reasons, try to take advantage of their teammates or the coach.

"Con men" are basically dishonest; that is, they use alibis, excuses or outright lies to make life easier for themselves. They may possess incredible powers of persuasion—which, if channeled properly, could make them excellent team leaders if only they could be trusted with responsibility—but they are likely to use those powers in ways that cause disharmony on the team and drive coaches to distraction. "Con men'" should be told in no uncertain terms what is desirable and undesirable in terms of their behavior and how they will be punished for rules violations.

Naturally, I prefer punishment to the finality of *dismissal* from the squad—but I do not rule out the latter.

Incidentally, Coach Larry Chapman, Head Basketball Coach at Auburn University/Montgomery, has an interesting theory about dismissing players from his teams:

> I never kick a player off my team (he told me). First of all, when a player becomes a behavior problem or breaks team rules, I'll take him aside and talk to him. If that doesn't straighten him out, I'll punish him. If his problem continues, I'll keep increasing the penalties until he either straightens up or decides to quit the team. But I won't kick him off.[2]
>
> If I kick him off, his parents, friends and even some of his teammates probably will be upset enough to blame me for it. But if he quits the team, there's nothing anyone can say to point a finger of guilt at me.

Can habitual rules breakers be saved? If so, Coach Chapman's graduated scale of punishment probably offers the best chance for the errant player's redemption. Punishment is, or can be, extremely effective in halting undesired behavior.[3] The player's learning what behaviors *are* desired is a function of communication between the player and the coach.

Sadly, no definitive answer exists to the question of whether the coach who has lost a player for the kinds of reasons we're talking about here, whether by the player's quitting or being dismissed from the squad, should encourage the player to return to the team at a later date. Should the coach ignore this troubled soul in the hope that he can straighten himself out and return to the team later? Should he wait for the player to come to him, or try to maintain a semblance of

---

[2]The single exception to this rule, Coach Chapman notes, is when a player is found to have violated the law. In such cases, he dismisses the player involved from the team immediately.

[3]The exception to this rule occurs when misbehavior results from the player's misguided search for *attention*. In such cases, punishment may actually be regarded by the player as a reward, since the punishment itself is a form of attention. Isolation from the group—and not attempting to ignore the offense—is the best form of punishment for players who misbehave to attract attention.

communication with the player during his absence? Having tried it both ways, I still have no solid evidence that either technique is superior to the other.

The team's best interests always come first, of course, above and beyond those of the player or the coach. And since I cherish the limited time and contact I have with my players, I prefer not to waste my time on players who cannot or will not change their behavior for the good of the team.

When a player announces that he/she is going to quit the team, I talk with the player at length, trying for one last time to impress upon the player the value as I see it of his or her remaining on the team. I never ask the player not to quit, though; I consider it demeaning to the player's intelligence as well as my own. And if, at the end of our discussion, the player still wants to quit, I carefully warn him/her that, once the decision is made and carried out, it's final. No deposit, no return.

Such an approach—admittedly hard-line—is painful for me to pursue. Still, it's the price I have to pay for having chosen such a demanding profession for my life's work. No one ever promised me a rose garden. I find that I can live with this kind of approach in terms of team stability more easily than spending months on end wondering and worrying if maybe I should have compromised myself and the team for the player's sake.

Hyperanxious, or Psyched-out, Athletes

Players of this sort do not handle pressure very well. Therefore, the coach should attempt to structure competitive situations of gradually increasing difficulty in which the athlete's confidence is bolstered initially by successes. This type of athlete must be brought along slowly. It is vital to the player's emotional development that the coach not set expectations too high, and that the coach communicate to the player precisely what those expectations are.

Success-Phobic Athletes

Strange as it may seem, some athletes are afraid to win or to achieve personal success in sports. The primary reason for occurrence of this strange phenomenon is the athlete's fear of jealousy, resentment or rejection, whether by teammates, fans, etc., resulting from the player's athletic successes. A quarterback doesn't want to call his own number and sneak the ball over the goal line from the one because he's afraid his teammates will think he's a glory hound trying to make the headlines; a player works himself free for an open shot in basketball or hockey, then inexplicably passes to a heavily guarded teammate rather than taking the shot himself. When asked why, the player explains, "I didn't want to get everyone mad at me."

The key to dealing with this problem is to clearly define roles. Every coach wants his/her best players controlling the ball or taking the best available shots in pressure situations. Many coaches carry this process even farther by carefully defining and delimiting their players' roles in terms of specialization. A basketball coach told me,

> I know coaches who think that every player is somehow enti-
> tled to the same number of shots every game, so they put in patterns
> that give everybody on the team, even the very weakest shooters, the
> same number of shooting opportunities. But I don't see anything
> wrong with having a game plan where my best shooters and ball-
> handlers control the ball at our end of the court most of the time. I
> think it's good percentage basketball.
>
> This is the era of specialization! I don't want my good rebound-
> er who can't handle the ball well dribbling around the court like
> Tiny Archibald! And if the kid can't shoot fish in a rain barrel, I'm
> not looking for him to put up crowd-pleasers from the balconies!
> What I want him to do is go out and get us a dozen or so rebounds
> and then fill his lane in our fast breaks.

Regarding our present problem, athletes who are afraid to risk peer disapproval or jealousy by dominating a phase of the game such as scoring or handling the ball, the coach should explain to the team as a whole, and to the individual in question as well, how the superior athlete's advanced skills require that he or she dominate certain phases of the action in order for the team as a whole to function best. The basketball coach previously cited explains,

> I tell my players, "Hey, if you want to score more points, work
> on a shot you can make, and I'll have you shooting so much your
> jersey sleeve will still be flopping a half-hour after the game is over!
> But if you can't shoot well enough to hit your open shots consis-
> tently, don't expect to shoot a lot, and don't gripe when I tell some-
> one else to shoot more often. Be content to do what you do best, and
> leave the rest of the skills to someone else."

Withdrawn or Suspicious Athletes

The withdrawn or suspicious athlete is likely to be a desperately unhappy person. People have violated his trust often enough in the past to have hurt him deeply, to the extent that he is willing to hide behind a wall of silence or suspicion most of the time.

It is vital that the coach maintain an open, honest relationship with withdrawn or suspicious athletes. A warm, concerned relationship with players away from the court or playing field is a definite plus for the coach in this regard. A friendly smile, an encouraging pat on the shoulder now and then, may be just what the athlete needs to begin to break down the barriers of mistrust that have grown in the athlete's mind over the years.

Another technique that some coaches have found to be successful in dealing with withdrawn athletes is for the coach to assign one or more players to take special pains to try to befriend the player in question. Many times, the player can more easily be drawn out of his shell through newfound friendships with one or more of his teammates than through any of the coach's personal efforts. As is true with most behavioral problems, however, the coach should not expect success to be immediately forthcoming. An attitude of mistrust built up over a period of years is not likely to vanish overnight.

Depression-Prone Athletes

In dealing with athletes who suffer periodic spells of depression, it helps to find out whether the depression is due to personal problems or concern over poor performances in recent games. Concerning the latter, the coach can help greatly in encouraging the athlete, offering advice and/or constructive criticism, and suggesting that the player concentrate on other aspects of his overall game until he works his way out of his slump.

Probably the best way to deal with player depression resulting from personal problems is to give the athlete the opportunity to talk at length about his problem. Even if no satisfactory solution can be reached, the athlete will leave the conference secure in the knowledge that the coach is concerned about him personally as well as athletically.

The coach may also want to arrange for the player to talk to others, such as the school counselor or the pastor of the player's church, if the situation warrants.

Malingerers

Malingerers are persons who pretend to be ill or otherwise incapacitated for the purpose of avoiding work. The malingerer knows that his "injury" is at worst extremely minor, if indeed it exists at all. Thus, he is closely akin to the "con man" described previously: he is trying to put something over on someone—his teammates or the coach—for his own benefit.

An associated problem in dealing with the malingerer is that he is like "the boy who cried wolf": his complaints are so frequent, and so plaintive, that the coach eventually begins to doubt whether *any* injury or illness suffered by the player in question is real.[4]

The malingerer must be made to see that the shortcuts he is trying to take aren't really shortcuts at all, except to mediocrity, and that he is cheating his teammates when he uses imaginary or exaggerated injuries to get out of work that his teammates must continue to perform without him. Malingerers require constant, close supervision and guidance. Without it, they seldom achieve even a fraction of their athletic potential.

Everyone has problems. Life itself is a series of problems, particularly for young people who haven't yet become experienced enough to deal with their problems in a meaningful, mature fashion. It helps to remind youngsters that neither their problems nor the frustration they feel in dealing with those problems is unique to them. It helps, too, for the coach to try to remember what it was like to be a scared, frustrated teenager. Such recollections give us a much-needed sense of compassion in dealing with young people.

The converse of this way of thinking should be made clear to problem players, too, namely, that we as coaches have problems (e.g., winning often enough to retain our coaching jobs) that we expect the player to help us solve. I think it helps a great deal to express a

---

[4]This particular bit of analysis applies equally to the *hypochondriac*, or person who is unduly concerned with the condition of his/her health.

willingness to work with youngsters concerning their personal problems, as long as they are willing to work with us on *our* problems. As Herschel Walker is fond of saying, "People helping people; that's what life is all about."

CHAPTER 17

Handling the "Superstar" Athlete

DEFINITION

First, let's define the term *superstar.* A superstar athlete is one who, by virtue of superior physical and/or mental skills, is consistently able to dictate or control the flow and outcomes of games, matches, or contests. The superstar is a clearly dominant performer on his/her level of competition, and is a "winner" in the sense that he/she functions as well or better in pressure-filled situations as in situations in which the outcome is no longer in question.

Every coach should have the opportunity to coach at least one bona fide superstar athlete in his/her career. Highly skilled, highly motivated athletes are a joy to coach—and they make winning so much easier, too! Get the ball to a Herschel Walker or a Ralph Sampson often enough in the course of a game, and wonderful things begin to happen sooner or later. Set a Renaldo "Skeets" Nehemiah or an Edwin Moses in the starting blocks for a hurdles race, and you're likely to witness an event that will stay fresh in your memory for as long as you live.

PREREQUISITES AND ADVANTAGES

In the course of 17 years of coaching, I've been fortunate enough to have coached three athletes who I thought qualified as authentic superstars at the time I coached them. Aside from their superior skills—the most obvious prerequisite for superstardom—these young athletes shared three common traits which relate directly or indirectly to motivation. First, they possessed an uncommonly high degree of competitive drive, self-discipline, and self-motivation. Second, they responded very well to instruction and were willing to work on new techniques without questioning on their part or prodding on my part. Third, they genuinely and wholeheartedly loved their respective sports.

While not every superstar athlete is as coachable as those I was associated with, there are many advantages to coaching such athletes, including the following:

1. *They can make you an instant (and consistent) winner.* Coaching superstar athletes is like teaching gifted classes: whatever you do is likely to work. In team sports, the presence of a superstar in the lineup tends to force opponents to play you differently than they would otherwise. They may have to make changes in their basic style of play in order to control the superstar's performance. And the farther a team strays from what it does best the less likely it is to be successful in controlling opponents.

2. *They tend to make everyone else on the team work harder and play more effectively.* If you're an offensive lineman blocking for an Earl Campbell or a Herschel Walker, for example, you don't have to open holes for them to run through: all they need is *half* a hole. They'll do the rest themselves, by breaking the arm tackles.

The knowledge that even a half-effective effort on your part is likely to make you look like an extremely proficient blocker should provide all the motivation you need to work as hard as you can to give your superstar that half-step he needs to clear the line and break a long run downfield. The presence of a superstar makes everyone on his/her team look better than they actually are.

3. *Generally (but not always), superstars tend to make good team leaders.* Such a role appears natural for them, since their less gifted

teammates naturally look to them for leadership whenever the going gets tough.

Still, the coach should not attempt to force superstars into leadership roles when they clearly do not want to function as team leaders, or when their performances suffer as a result of their assuming leadership roles they do not want.

4. *The presence of one or more superstar athletes can bring publicity and recognition to your program.* Media attention is naturally drawn to superior players. (It was, in fact, the media who invented and popularized the concept of superstars.) Increased exposure of your athletes to public notice always has a highly desirable positive effect on your total program.

5. *You have to work to stay ahead of the superstar in your coaching.* This can be an advantage or disadvantage, depending upon your viewpoint. I consider it an advantage. I believe that coaches should always work hard, although not all of them do.

6. *Ordinarily, superstars do not require much in the way of external motivation, since they tend to be highly motivated already.* The exception to this rule is the enormously gifted athlete who takes his/her skills for granted and has no desire to improve his/her performance through practice or proper conditioning.

For the most part, though, you have little or nothing to worry about in dealing with your superior athletes. Most of them want to excel, and to win, just as much as you do.

7. *The superstar athlete functions well in pressure situations— sometimes even better than the coach.* Rudyard Kipling wrote, "If you can keep your head while those about you/Are losing theirs . . ." His words perfectly describe the superstars. They don't "choke," because they're used to operating under pressure. *Every* situation is a pressure situation for them, because they're always expected to perform at high levels of proficiency.

President Harry Truman was once asked how he was able to withstand the awesome pressures of the Presidency. Mr. Truman replied, "If you can't take the heat, get out of the kitchen." Well, your superstars *can* take the heat; they've proven it time and again in the process of building their superlative skills. *You* may wilt under the pressures to win when the game is on the line, but your superstar will take it in stride and function in the best manner possible. That's precisely why he/she *is* a superstar.

TURNING PROBLEMS INTO ADVANTAGES

Coaching is seldom easy. If it were otherwise, the sports world already would be overrun with great coaches. And although I've stressed the joys of working with highly talented athletes, there may be some drawbacks to work out, too. The important thing to remember at this point, however, is that you can anticipate most of the problems and come to terms with them before they grow into major stumbling blocks to success in your program.

1. *The "superstar" concept may not fit into your concept of how the game should be played.* (I felt this way myself until I had my first superstar athlete, after which my philosophy of coaching changed faster than a politician's promises.)

Basically, the question is, Do you want a superstar carrying most of the load (and getting most of the publicity), or do you want a broader and more diversified style of play in which everyone shares the spotlight and the work load? Without going deeper into the reasons underlying these viewpoints, there are two approaches you can take to the problem:

(a) You can "Let The Big Dog run," so to speak, as University of Georgia fans referred to Coach Vince Dooley's use of I-back Herschel Walker; or

(b) You can incorporate the superstar into your present style of play, which is pretty much what Coach Darrell Royal did with Earl Campbell at the fullback position in the University of Texas's wishbone offense. Dean Smith has done the same thing repeatedly in his highly successful basketball program at the University of North Carolina.

Either technique can work, granted two provisions: *you* have to believe that your decision reflects what is best for your team, and you must convince your players—the superstar *and* his/her teammates—that your decision is best for them. If you can do that, you're on your way, and heaven help the people who have to play against you!

2. *Coaching superstars can make you a lazy coach.* If, that is, you were lazy in the first place. But you'd have a hard time finding coaches who would tell you that John Wooden took it easy when he coached

that incredible string of superstars at UCLA who won ten NCAA championships in twelve years between 1964–1975. I've had coaches tell me, "*Anybody* could win with all the talented players *he* had." Don't you believe it, though. The only way you or I could have come close to equalling Wooden's accomplishments with the same players is by working just as hard as he did to blend their skills into a winning combination—and even then most of us would fail to match his skills as a teacher and a tactician.

UCLA basketball during that period came as close as humanly possible to ideal: *a superstar coach coaching superstar athletes.*

In discussing the football coaching career of Alabama's Paul Bryant, Coach Jake Gaither of Florida A & M gave the Bear perhaps the finest compliment one coach can give another when he said of Bryant, "He can take his'n and beat your'n, or take your'n and beat his'n." Now, *that's* coaching!

3. *The danger always exists that your superstar may become a prima donna who expects special treatment.* This problem—or, more accurately, its likelihood—is due in part to the fact that you *will* treat your superstars differently, simply because they *are* different. Their motivations are different—deeper, in most cases—and the results they achieve certainly defy comparison with those of their less talented peers. Too, the fact that so many outstanding athletes today are youngsters from under-privileged backgrounds may hinder their ability to handle the deluge of publicity they receive. Finally, we have to remember that, for the most part, these are immature teenagers who are constantly being reminded by the media that they are God's gift to athletics. How many times does a youngster have to hear that he/she is a superstar before the youngster starts to believe it and act accordingly?

THE SPECIAL TREATMENT PROBLEM—
CONSIDERATIONS AND GUIDELINES

1. Don't *try* to treat the superstar athlete differently from your other players. If it happens naturally, don't worry about it. And don't apologize for it. Sure, you're going to treat your superstar differently—but not in terms of what you expect from him/her in the way of attitude and behavior.

2. In light of all that has been said thus far in this chapter, it should come as no great surprise to find that I consider *communication* to be the key to dealing effectively with superstar athletes. To you (and to their teammates), at least, they're just ordinary young people with extraordinary skills. You should attempt to transmit to them in as many ways as possible your expectations and personal concern for their well-being. You want them to feel a sense of obligation to you and the team to live up to what is expected of them—but is this really any different from what you want from every player?

You should not be afraid to criticize your superstar athlete when situations arise that warrant criticism. Constructive criticism is a necessary part of the learning process, and no one—not even superstars or their coaches—should be held in such high esteem that their skills or efforts (or lack of effort) are beyond question or criticism. You should not have to live in fear of offending your players, including the superstar athlete. If they're athletes—real athletes, that is—they can take it. But you can't carry them on a splinter, pretending that everything is all right. That's the best way in the world to make large problems out of small ones.

I've never believed in letting problems fester unresolved in the hope that things will get better if left alone. As coach, a large part of my job consists of solving problems, and I prefer to confront problems openly and directly before they grow into major problems. When I see a potentially bad situation developing, whether with a superstar athlete or anyone else connected with the team, I take the player(s) aside and discuss the problem to whatever length is necessary to resolve the problem to the player's and my satisfaction.

It's important for the extraordinary athlete to understand that superior performances involve skills *and* effort, and not skills alone. In communicating with your superstar athlete in this regard, you may want to point out Jesus' words:

> For unto whomsoever much is given, of him shall much be required; and to whom men have committed much, of him will they ask the more.
>
> Luke 12:48

You can't say it any better than that: twenty-six words encompassing all that every superior athlete needs to know about obligation and responsibility.

Even superstar athletes must be told, and then reminded periodically, that their ability is a gift for which they should be thankful. Although I have no desire to inflict my religious views on anyone except to illustrate my point, I believe it is a sin to take one's talents for granted, or to waste them by not working to fulfill one's potential, whether in athletics or in any other phase of life.

We've all seen gifted athletes who, for one reason or another, never reached their potential. And while the coach may or may not be a factor in this process, depending upon the individual and the situation, you as coach should do your utmost to become a factor by attempting to exert a positive influence on that player's life. You may not reach the unreachable star athlete, but giving your best effort on that player's behalf exemplifies precisely the attitude you want that player to have.

3. Define as clearly as possible the roles of every player on your team, and let it be known to all concerned that no one on the team will be permitted to question those roles.

In this regard, it should prove helpful for you to spend time working with, and talking to, other players as well as your superstar. You should make an effort to show an interest in all of your players, and to stress the importance of their own contributions as well as those of the team's superstar. Such concern on your part for every player as an important factor in the team's success will go far toward eliminating jealousy as a potentially divisive force affecting your team. Too, clearly defining every player's role will kill two birds with one stone, as it were, by showing the players that winning or losing is a *team* function. You do not want your superstar or his/her teammates to feel that the responsibility for winning or losing rests in the hands of one or two key players. Nothing productive is likely to result from that sort of attitude.

4. If necessary, temper your praise with criticism, or else limit your praise. I prefer the former tactic, since (a) the superstars can take the heat, and (b) players always should be recognized for superior performances.)

While a positive atmosphere is generally conducive to learning, some players require constant prodding to keep them on top of their game.

5. Don't let your superstar athlete take himself/herself too seriously. If, like me, you coach in a primarily rural setting, you'll perhaps understand the fine line between working hard to have your superstar's

efforts publicized in the city newspapers and working hard to keep your superstar from believing everything that's written about him/her. As media attention increases, you may find your superstar developing a "super-ego" (not in the Freudian sense). There are several ways you can deal with this.

First, you should continually stress *team* accomplishments, and place added emphasis on the efforts of players other than your superstar. Second, you might devise techniques for telling or showing your superior player how the rest of the team contributes to his/her success. (In football, for example, coaches traditionally have humbled cocky backs by instructing the offensive linemen not to block for them on a given sequence of plays.)

Third, you can joke about the superstar's glowing headlines or writeups. (I like to read them aloud to the whole team, adding comments such as "Does anyone here seriously believe that? That guy ought to write for the funny pages!" I've kidded my superstars about having bad breath or flat feet, or being ugly, or fat or skinny—in short, about any shortcomings humans might have that might remind them that they are, after all, "human, all too human.")

When I began writing this section, I underestimated its importance within the overall context of motivation. As I wrote, however, I gradually began to realize that I wasn't discussing superstars as much as *superior athletes*, regardless of whether or not they're called superstars. I realized, too, that this section perhaps has as much to do with player and team relationships as any other section in the entire book, for one very important reason:

IN ORDER TO CONTROL YOUR TEAM, YOU MUST CONTROL YOUR BEST PLAYERS.

You must control the way your players think, and feel, and act—and unless you can control your superior athletes in this regard, you will never command the respect or confidence of the rest of your players.

Fortunately, most superior athletes are self-disciplined and internally motivated, which tends to make them easy to work with. Still, your motivational efforts should be directed primarily toward those players who will be responsible for winning or losing: if you cannot inspire your best players to their best efforts, you may not win regardless of how charged up the rest of the players are.

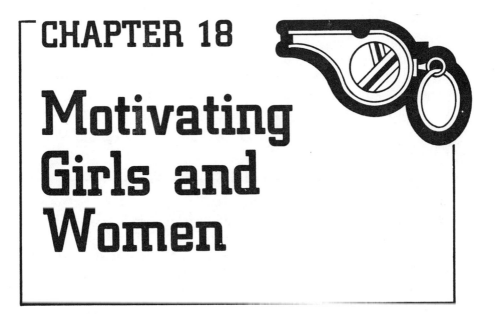

CHAPTER 18

Motivating Girls and Women

In seventeen years of coaching, I've had the opportunity to coach young men and women in a variety of sports. The empirical conclusion I've reached is that, with all other factors being equal, women are easier to motivate than men. For me, at least, the most difficult aspect of coaching women has been to teach them to overcome their natural tendency to respond as women rather than as athletes.

THE STEREOTYPED WOMAN ATHLETE

In our society, girls have traditionally been discouraged from participating in strenuous physical activities that build muscular strength and endurance. And while it is true "we've come a long way, baby," in changing the image of women as dainty, fragile creatures whose only proper strenuous physical activity is that of giving birth, our society has not yet become so liberated that girls are encouraged from the very beginning of their existences to develop athletic physiques or powerful musculature. A large segment of our population, both men and women, still prefers women to be *feminine* rather than *female*. I do not intend to take sides in this argument, except to note that, in sports, the athletes will beat the non-athletes every time.

And that's the crux of the problem I've faced in coaching women. They want to be athletes, but in so many cases either (a) their boyfriends don't want them to, (b) they're afraid they'll develop large, unsightly (to them) muscles, or (c) their background in organized big-muscle activity has not prepared them physically or psychologically to accept the rigorous physical training necessary for effective athletic participation.

CHANGING THE STEREOTYPE

The year before I came to Toombs Central High School, the girls basketball team had a 6'0" senior center, a 5'10", 165-lb. junior forward, and a 5'9" freshman ballhandler who later played at Mercer University—and TC won only 4 games while losing 19 that year! Although the school had had some fine girls' basketball teams in the distant past, recent years had brought nothing but losing seasons—12 wins and 76 losses in the four years prior to my arrival—and team morale was understandably low. But that didn't matter; *my* morale was high: we had a 5'10", 165-lb. center who I thought was an *athlete* (looks can be deceiving, can't they?), a good 5'9" ballhandler who would someday play college basketball, and six other letter winners returning! Besides, I had a lifetime mark of 126 wins and only 20 losses; there was just *no way* we could lose!

Three girls walked out the first day when I announced that we were going to run a mile every day before we started practice. Two girls (letter-winners, of course) decided to pass up their senior season to devote themselves to married life. Three more decided that they'd rather not play on the same team with blacks. (It was the first year after the school was integrated, and three blacks were trying out for the team. All three made the squad.)

We were left with seven players to suit up to play six-girl basketball—and one of the players was a Seventh-Day Adventist who couldn't play on Saturdays. No one on the team had ever been expected to hustle before—the 5'10" center covered the corner in our zone defense by stamping her foot at the shooter, shouting "Shoot!," and clapping her hands together loudly to distract the shooter. No one had any idea what a *real* basketball practice was like, and consequently no one knew what an honest effort was like in games, either.

We won seven games that year. The girls were totally incapable of handling pressure, since they'd seldom had any pressure on them in the past. (The previous year's 4–19 squad had lost by an average of 19.4 ppg.) My reaction was to keep pressure on them every second of practices through endless repetition of competitive drills involving rewards and punishment, constantly forcing them to increase the level of intensity of their performances, shouting, pleading, reasoning, cajoling, joking, and even praying with them to understand the importance of giving your best in everything you do.

I never gave the girls a second's rest. I ran with them in the gym, mile after mile, and even ran "bleachers" (up the bleachers, touch the wall, back down, etc.) with them. I worked hard enough that year to deserve *three* years' worth of coaching supplements, but all I had to show for it at the end of the year were 7 wins, 12 losses, and a small band of "survivors"—that's what we called ourselves—who were beginning to resemble basketball players. I didn't know at the time how much pride the girls had built, since all I had for evidence was the losers' statistics of having won seven games rather than the previous year's four, and losing by an average of 2.5 ppg. rather than by 19.4 ppg.

Over the next five years, though, we won 93 games while losing only 28—and we never finished lower than third in our Region after that 7–12 season.

Treating Players as Athletes, Not Women

I've never wanted blacks or whites on my teams: I've always wanted *athletes*. And I don't want to coach girls or women; I want to coach *athletes*. Sure, obvious differences exist between men and women—men don't get pregnant or undergo menstrual periods—but the coach, whether male or female, who treats his/her players as women first and athletes second is mistaking priorities. I'm a husband, a Methodist, a writer, a (terrible) fisherman, for example—*but not when I'm coaching my teams!* Then, I'm a coach first, and everything else I am is of secondary importance.

In like manner, a women's coach has both the right and the obligation to expect his/her players to forego other roles and interests when they are practicing or performing in their particular sport. Female athletes should not be permitted to perform in practice or in games in a "ladylike" manner.

The Differences Between the Sexes

The greatest differences between the sexes in terms of athletic performance, Carole Baumgarten (1976, p. 16) notes, are the level of skills and the level of competitiveness. While boys are trained from early childhood to be competitive, Baumgarten notes, girls may be concerned with such athletically nonessential factors as keeping their hair straight while playing. Baumgarten suggests using competitive drills constantly as a means of developing a competitive attitude in girls.

The other side of the coin is that, while males are directed toward competitiveness more often, and at an earlier age, than females in our society, the fact that competition is relatively new to women can also work in the coach's favor: once a pattern of competitive behavior has been established, women are likely to enjoy their new-found interest in athletic participation even more than men. And because women have traditionally been permitted (or expected) to display their emotions rather than keeping them bottled up, the coach is likely to receive immediate feedback that will help in judging the effectiveness of his or her motivational attempts—providing, of course, that the coach is able to correctly interpret the players' responses.

MOTIVATING GIRLS AND WOMEN

A high school boys' basketball coach had his players fill out a questionnaire during preseason practice, one of the questions of which was "Why are you playing basketball?" One player, a third-string sophomore who later quit school midway through his senior year, wrote, "I wont (sic) to play in the NBA."

A women's professional basketball league presently exists, but few if any girls on the high school or junior high school level play basketball for the expressed purpose of making it in the pro leagues later on. Opportunities for participation in women's athletics at the college level have expanded drastically in recent years, due in no small measure to Title IX rulings, but the majority of girls participating in junior high and high school team sports are not motivated primarily by the desire to receive athletic scholarships, or by dreams of someday becoming a professional athlete. Most young women playing in team sports at the high school level expect to fill other roles after graduation— housewives, mothers, career women, etc.—rather than continuing their athletic careers into the collegiate or professional ranks.

Taking all of the preceding into consideration, then—that women do not receive the impetus toward competition that men receive in the early years of their development, and that women are not as likely to be motivated toward participating in athletics after graduation—*what is the best way to motivate girls and women?*

The answer was given in Chapter 7: "The best motivator is LOVE." Women have always been better at expressing love than men. Women are not bound by macho images ("a man's man") or concepts of masculine behavior ("big boys don't cry"). Women are permitted to touch each other without fear of societal disapproval; they hug when meeting, hold hands while talking and kiss each other goodbye.

Men, on the other hand, may shake hands in greeting or farewell, but more prolonged intimate physical contact between two men is generally considered to be socially unacceptable in our society except in times of deep emotion, as in expressing love and condolence to a close relative or friend in a time of grief, or winning an important game in sport.

Physical contact binds people together emotionally as well as physically. Depending upon the context in which it occurs, touching can relay a message of rejection, sympathy, friendship, sincerity, playfulness, dislike, or virtually any other human emotion. In athletics, contact between teammates can symbolize love, acceptance and commitment. It is not at all uncommon for basketball players to touch their hands together before leaving their huddle during time outs; some football teams (e.g., the Pittsburgh Steelers) have even held hands during their defensive huddles. In such cases, the physical contact symbolizes the individual players' commitment to the group or team. And because women have always been more contact-oriented than men, I think the coach in women's sports can and should encourage this kind of contact. It expresses love, loyalty, friendship and team ties in ways that words could never accomplish. In my experience, at least, it's the most powerful motivational device a coach can use.

The "Touch" Rule

In my second year of coaching girls basketball at Toombs Central, we started out with a squad of fifteen players divided into about four cliques, none of which had much to do with the others. The players in each clique were more or less loyal to each other, but not to the team. To combat this state of misplaced loyalty, I installed a rule that, whenever any player met or passed a teammate (or me) in the halls, library, lunchroom, locker room, or anywhere else on campus during the school day, both of them (or us, in my case) would extend a hand for a simple touch. That touch, I explained, was a symbol of our acceptance of each other; if anyone was unwilling either to accept me or her teammates, or to "fake" such acceptance by complying with the rule—well, we would have to do without her services on our team that year. And to make sure that everyone understood the importance I placed on the rule, I set an automatic penalty of an extra mile of running at practice for every intentional offense. I included myself in the agreement, and gave them three days to practice the procedure before the rule went into effect.

I had bus duty in the mornings before school, so I saw every player as she arrived. If I was busy, players would wait by the buses until I was free: they preferred avoiding that extra mile of running at practice more than they disliked touching my hand or their teammates' hands. (If a girl simply didn't see her teammate or me, no penalty was imposed—but if she passed me in the halls without looking, I'd call her over to touch hands.)

I was not, of course, interested in physical contact *per se* (although I have since been told of a male junior high coach who carried the process to the rather dubious extreme of requiring *embraces* from his girls); rather, I wanted the players to feel that (a) I accepted them, (b) their teammates accepted them, and (c) they had a reciprocal responsibility and commitment to accept their teammates, and me as well.

Results

In five years, we had a total of seven instances in which girls had to run an extra mile at practice for flagrant failure to touch hands. Five of those occasions arose during the first week the rule was in force. And while the experience of touching hands was embarrassing to all of us for a day or two, we got over it in a short time. I am convinced that, although many other factors were involved, the "touch rule" was the major reason we were able to turn a losing program around completely in only two years. The cliques vanished immediately: almost without exception, the girls not merely tolerated, but actually *enjoyed*, their wholesale acceptance by the rest of their teammates.

We had only one related problem develop during the years in which I employed the touch rule at TC: my co-captains came to me one day saying that they had a problem with one of our new players, a transfer student. "We like the touch rule, Coach," one of them said, "but Janice is driving us crazy! She waits outside our rooms between classes to touch our hands, and she chases us down the hall or comes all the way across the lunchroom to touch hands every time she sees us."

"I've touched Janice's hand twelve times already today," the other girl joined in, "and it's only third period!"

I explained to the girls that Janice (not her real name) needed a sense of belonging and acceptance, and that *that* was why we'd started using the touch rule in the first place. "She's doing the same thing to me." I said, "but it's a cross we'll have to bear."

Janice later transferred to a neighboring school and made their basketball team. While we were warming up for them the next year, Janice left her team's layup line and ran down to our end of the court to touch hands with everyone on our team. I heard one of our co-captains grumble, "I'll bet she's been waiting all year to do that."

She probably had. And that's why I'm such a firm believer in it.

CHAPTER 19

Motivating Your Reserves and Benchwarmers

BENCHWARMERS—A KEY TO TEAM MORALE

In our concern with finding suitable starting lineups and front line substitutes, we coaches sometimes overlook the potential for contribution to team goals by lesser skilled players on the squad who don't get much playing time. Such an oversight can have grave implication for team morale. Conversely, making every player feel that he/she is contributing in a meaningful way to team goals is likely to pay handsome dividends. Coach Dave DeVenzio (1980, p. 78) contended that having benchwarmers with good attitudes virtually guarantees that the regulars will have good attitudes, too.

The problem is, of course, that seldom-used players are likely to resent their lack of playing time, and their resentment can create discord and disharmony on the team. On the college or pro level, the problem is amplified by the fact that virtually all of the players are used to having played regularly at lower levels of play.

Dean Smith's Strategy: Making Every Minute Count

University of North Carolina Basketball Coach Dean Smith uses a "Blue" team composed of third-stringers who otherwise might receive little or no playing time. These players, spelling the regulars and front line subs for 2–3 minutes at a time, play with an intensity that is truly amazing to watch. Possessing a nickname denied the first two teams, "Blue" team members take considerable pride in their ability to come in cold and not only to keep the Tarheels in games, but in many cases to catch up or extend the team's lead. Coach Smith is as likely to put in his "Blue" team in pressure situations as when the team is far ahead or hopelessly behind. "Blue" team players know and respect this, and they routinely give some of the finest efforts in all of college basketball to justify Coach Smith's faith in them.

This technique undoubtedly helps Coach Smith in his recruiting, too, since basketball prospects know that they aren't going to spend four years at UNC with their posteriors welded to the bench. You may not consider recruiting an important concern if you're a high school or junior high coach; still, increasing the playing time of your benchwarmers can help to draw new players from your school into your program.

When Basketball Coach Richard "Digger" Phelps incorporated this technique with his Notre Dame teams a few years ago, his third-stringers not only eagerly embraced the idea, but their elected captain took over their coaching in practices and ran them through extra conditioning drills and called extra or extended practice sessions when he—the captain, not Coach Phelps—decided that they needed additional work.

RECOGNITION AND TREATMENT OF RESERVE PLAYERS

Along with giving benchwarmers the opportunity for a certain amount of playing time, the prudent coach will attempt to publicly recognize his/her marginal players as well as the regulars. This recognition may be in the form of comments to the press or student journalists representing the school newspaper, recognition at pep rallies, or announcing selected subs instead of the starters during pre-game introductions. Or, Coach Dave DeVenzio (1980, p. 78) explained, the coach can introduce the entire squad.

Coach DeVenzio also suggested that the coach should tell all of his/her players what they're doing wrong, rather than simply making positive comments, overlooking mistakes or correcting only the starters. Along with this, I think it's important that, when a game is for all practical purposes already won or lost, the coach not merely send in the scrubs and sit back and watch the game to its conclusion. Players, whether regulars or substitutes, should always be expected to give their best effort on the field or court. They should never be ignored, regardless of the game's outcome.

You can also use game situations as teaching situations for your subs, by explaining to players on the bench what went wrong (or right) on a given play and why, along with how such situations can be either avoided or created.

Finally, it's important to remind young, unskilled players of the necessity of "paying their dues" by accepting secondary roles until they acquire the skills necessary for increased playing time. Being up front with the players promotes mutual respect, and in the case of marginal players such private talks enhance the players' sense of belonging and self-identity.

In the words of the blind English poet John Milton (1608–74), "They also serve who only stand and wait."

CHAPTER 20

Handling Your Assistant Coaches

The key to good relationships with your assistant coaches—and to motivating them, as well—is contained in a single word: *professionalism.* If you are professional in your dealings with your assistants, only two kinds of problems are likely to be serious: *covetousness* (e.g., an assistant coach who is after your job), and *immaturity* (e.g., a young assistant just out of college who still thinks and believes as a teenager rather than as an adult).

PROBLEM COACHES

In the case of covetousness, the dissatisfied assistant is likely to do everything he can to undercut your authority with the players, second-guess (loudly!) every decision you make, and generally make life miserable for you so you'll leave and *he* can take over. Immediate dismissal of the unruly assistant may be out of the question; you may have to grin and bear it until such time as he can be replaced. Meanwhile, you should show no concern over the coach's actions, and strive to demonstrate the highest brand of professionalism possible in your dealings with him. (Of course, you could also take him out behind the gym for some one-on-one, but that's hardly a professional response, even if it would be emotionally satisfying.)

Once you have determined that an assistant is disloyal to you and does not have the team's best interests at heart, you should reduce his responsibilities and endeavor to keep him as far away from the action as possible—for example, by sending him on errands or giving him busy work to do during practice, giving him the day off from practice whenever feasible, sending him on scouting trips on game days instead of having him accompany the team, and/or whatever else may occur to you.

Concerning immaturity, you may be able to speed up the assistant coach's maturation by setting an example of professional conduct worthy of emulation—which is probably what you're doing already. Talking with the assistant about his behavior should help, too—or at least it should serve to make him more aware of behaving responsibly instead of smoking or drinking in front of (or with) the players, indulging in horseplay such as wrestling with the players, dating high school students, or whatever the young assistant's immaturity leads him to do.

NINE GUIDELINES FOR MOTIVATING
YOUR ASSISTANT COACHES

1. *Permit them to contribute in a meaningful way.* Give them definite responsibilities, not busy work or menial tasks that you wouldn't do yourself. Outline those responsibilities thoroughly. (If the job doesn't already have a specific title, you may want to give it one, and to prepare a written job scription as well.)

2. *Set a good example for them.* Work harder than your assistants. The reasons for this should be obvious.

3. *Set high expectations* for them. For example, you have every right to expect and require that they be on time, properly dressed and fully prepared for practices, games, team and coaches' meetings, etc. Expect them to shoulder their share of the load without complaint or excuse. If they're serious about coaching, they won't mind hard work or long hours.

4. *Communicate with them.* Ask their advice; listen; and evaluate. You don't have to follow your assistants' suggestions in every case, but you should be willing to listen and evaluate—and to use their advice if it is sound, or explain to them how or why their advice is unsound.

5. *Include your assistants in your strategy sessions and the decision-making process, whether as contributors or as learners.* In his strategy sessions, the late President John F. Kennedy used to seek out the views of each of his advisors, listen carefully and patiently as they expressed their opinions, ask them questions to clarify any misunderstandings, and then make his decisions based on his own viewpoint as well as his advisors' ability to defend their particular views. You may or may not want to go this far in soliciting your assistants' advice concerning strategy and tactics, depending upon their knowledge of the sport and the amount of faith you have in their judgment.

If you decide not to use a particular piece of advice or strategy suggested by an assistant coach, you should take time after the game to explain to the coach why his/her advice was not used. Otherwise, the coach is likely to decide that his/her advice is not needed.

If an assistant happens to be young and inexperienced, you can teach him how to evaluate game situations by discussing them with him as they arise or in post-game talks. Talking shop and providing access to learning resources can serve several useful purposes not only for your assistant coaches, but for other coaches on lower levels whose feeder programs provide players for your own program. You can conduct mini-clinics for these coaches, showing them how to teach fundamentals or patterns; you can provide books or other resources from your own coaching library for them to study; you can simply meet together regularly—say, once a week at a local steak house, for fellowship and the opportunity to talk shop and possibly transmit bits of your philosophy to the coaches (They can't complain if you, the Athletic Department or the Booster Club is footing the bill); or you can get together after games to rehash the game's high and low points.

These kinds of things may seem totally unimportant to you—but they may mean a world of difference to the other coaches involved.

One further point: you may want to give your inexperienced assistant coach the opportunity to call plays or defenses in football, or select strategy in other sports—but be advised that your good intentions can backfire if the moment is inopportune.

6. *Don't blame your assistant coaches for defeats.* Whenever Bear Bryant assessed blame for poor Crimson Tide performances, he always said that "we" did a poor job of getting the players ready. He never singled out individual players or coaches (except himself) for public criticism.

7. *Share the credit for victories.* If one were to believe the Bear, he was just a plain ol' country boy who, after nearly 40 years in the coaching business, was still so ignorant that his smart assistant coaches had to do all his thinking for him. No one believed that, of course— but that's one of many reasons why Bear's assistants always were so fiercely loyal to him.

One of the qualities that helped Coach Bryant to reach the pinnacles of success in the coaching ranks was that coaching was never an ego trip for him. For many of us, all we need is a few minutes in the limelight and we start hamming it up like Hollywood Henderson. For the Bear, though, the limelight and publicity were helpful only in terms of getting boys from places as far away as Pennsylvania and Hawaii to play football at Alabama. Other than that, one suspects that Coach Bryant could have done very nicely without all the hoopla and fanfare surrounding his victories, thank you!

8. *Try to avoid criticizing your assistant coaches in public, or correcting them in front of the players.* Sometimes it may have to be done, as in dealing with an immature person who persists in juvenile behavior that is unbecoming to, or undesirable for, a coach. Still, it's better to take the person aside and talk to him in private about the problem than to air your complaints in public. And *never* let players criticize an assistant coach.

9. *Back up decisions made by your assistant coaches. Don't take the player's side in confrontations.* Hopefully, of course, it won't come to that sort of impasse. If you ever have to make such a choice, though, professionalism dictates that you side with your assistant coach, regardless of whether he's right or not. You can always point out his error to him later, when the two of you are alone and away from the player(s) involved.

What you're trying to avoid here is having your athletes play you against your assistant coaches. When you were a child and you wanted to go to the park three blocks away, you asked your Mom if it was all right for you to go by yourself. If she said no, you went to your Dad and asked him the same question, only you mumbled so he couldn't exactly hear what you were asking. Sometimes he'd say yes, just to get rid of you and your persistent questions, and away you'd go. And when you got back later and Mom was ready to get a tree limb to you, you'd come out with your surefire, argument-stopping zinger: "But *Dad* said it was okay . . ."

CHAPTER 21

Five Seasons and Three Teams

Coach Hubie Brown, present head basketball coach of the New York Knicks has divided the sport season[1] into four distinct and separate phases, contending that teams tend to play differently as they move through the season from phase to phase.

In the present section, we'll use a modified version of Coach Brown's theory (with five seasons instead of four) to find out how teams of varying ability approach their games in terms of attitude.

Since it isn't possible to define the exact point where one phase of the season gives way to the next, let us approximate Coach Brown's four phases as follows: *the beginning of the season*, encompassing the first quarter of the season (in terms of the total number of regular season games to be played); *the middle of the season*, involving the middle 50 percent of regular season games; *the end of the regular season*, or the last quarter of the regular season; and *the playoffs*.

And to this we'll add a fifth, and probably most crucial season of all: pre-season practice.

---

[1]Any sport.

THE BEGINNING OF THE SEASON

All teams start out even before the season starts, at least, as far as their records are concerned. This is an important point to bear in mind because every player, even those on teams that will lose every game that season, is ready to play and hoping for an outstanding season.

The first few games are vitally important in setting the team's attitude for the rest of the season. Strong teams that are used to winning will have little trouble maintaining a winning attitude early, except when that part of their schedule is exceedingly difficult and they lose several games they were expected to win. In such cases, the coach should carefully point out that the team is, in fact, undergoing a particularly difficult period, and tell the players when they can start expecting to find light at the end of the tunnel. Concentrating on future goals can serve to reduce the bitterness of present disappointments.

Another strategy the coach might use in certain cases is to minimize the importance of losses to non-conference foes. This is particularly important in the earliest stages of the season when many teams play the majority of their non-conference contests, and when even strong teams still may be searching for their team identity.

Weak teams, particularly those which have been weak in the past, may have little or no difficulty in assuming their identities. Although their play may be inspired in the earliest stages of the season, they are likely to understand that their role is to lose so that others may win. This is precisely where coaching comes in: if you're in a new coaching situation where losing is a way of life, you may be able to fool yourself into thinking that, because you've never had a losing season before, it just can't happen to you now. It's like the man who fell off the top of a 100-story building: as he passed the twentieth floor on his way down he was heard to remark, "This isn't as bad as I'd thought it would be."

But your players know otherwise. They've been there, and they know just how bad it's likely to get. In the first few games, though, their level of motivation is likely to be high, as will be their receptivity to your efforts to motivate them.

Average teams—those that win somewhere between 40–60 percent of their games in the season's early stages—can go either way. If your team has a 2–3 record after your first five games, for example, you're only one game below .500. The players' confidence may or may not be as great as teams with 5–0 or 4–1 marks, but a winning season is still a viable, even *likely*, possibility for them. Thus, they normally should respond favorably to your motivational efforts.

THE MIDDLE OF THE SEASON

The middle half of the season is the phase in which: strong teams grow stronger, with their confidence (and thus their receptivity to motivation) growing with every win; weak teams tend to fall short of victory with increasing regularity, regardless of the coach's efforts to motivate them; and average teams continue to rise and fall with the calibre of their competition and their own level of motivation.

The strong team's greatest problem during this phase of the season is likely to be one of overconfidence, which means that the coach who relies on his/her players' being naturally self-motivated for every game is likely to be upset by a team of even average ability.

As before, the average team tends to rise to occasional upsets and fall prey to occasional upsets as well, dependent upon both the quality of its opponents and the coach's ability to control the players' attitudes.

Weak teams continue to lose most of the time because it's expected of them, like death and taxes.

Still, this is precisely where many coaches miss the mark concerning what motivation is all about. If you base your team's success primarily on whether it wins or not, and it loses, and loses, and loses—well, how else are your players to view themselves except as losers and failures?

Earlier, I described weak teams as *losers*. I did so, not because I consider them to be losers, but because they usually consider themselves to be losers. And in too many cases, their coaches do, too. Likewise their fans. And, perhaps most telling of all, so do their opponents. It soon becomes a seemingly endless downward spiral of negative expectations for the players from everyone they meet. Is it any wonder that they grow harder to motivate as the season wears on, when not even their own coach views them in positive terms?

A friend told me recently that he and his wife invited another couple over for an evening of bridge. The men paired up against their wives, and promptly proceeded to steal practically every bid the whole evening. The women were furious. "It's just not right!," one of the wives protested. "When we have the good hands, we should be allowed to play them!"

Too many coaches feel that, when they have the better team, the other team should roll over and lose quietly—and conversely, when theirs is the weaker team, they know in their heart of hearts that their opponents deserve to win. (After all, is there any disgrace in losing to a better team?) Still, I cannot conceive of any coach worthy of the name giving up, or letting his or her players admit defeat beforehand, simply because the opponent is stronger and has a better record.

When I came to Toombs Central and inherited a team that had gone many moons since its last winning season, I soon found myself unpopular with certain other coaches on our schedule. For a long time I had no idea why they disliked me, until finally it dawned on me that, for the first time in several years, those coaches were having to work to beat Toombs Central. We lost 12 of 19 games that first year, but not by lopsided scores. Some of the coaches whose teams we played resented the fact that we were losing to them by only one or two points instead of the 20–25 point shellackings they were used to hanging on us.

The middle of the season normally contains a great deal of drudgery and repetition in practice as teams continue with drills they started working on in pre-season and add seemingly endless repetitions of new and old patterns. The prudent coach will vary the drills and activities at least occasionally to prevent staleness and boredom from setting in, and he/she might consider adding a limited number of "fun" activities to the practice schedule every now and then during this phase of the season. After all, somewhere between 25–50 percent of the season still lies ahead, and the playoffs are still too far away to be a factor in motivation except in terms of seedings for tournament play.

THE END OF THE REGULAR SEASON

Often, by the time the end of the regular season rolls around, the outcomes of games are likely to be determined, not by which team is going to win, but by who's going to lose. It's been a long season, and there are precious few surprises left in the coach's and players' bag of tricks. Mental staleness is often a problem as teams go through the motions of games preordained to success or failure in the minds of everyone involved. The strong teams coast to victory after victory by virtue of their skills, the average teams still experience exciting victories and disappointing losses, and the weak teams find ways to lose to both.

It isn't always this way, of course—as, for example, when two strong teams meet (in which case little or no external motivation is needed)—but it's a common enough scenario near the end of the season.

Strong teams need to be motivated near the end of the season to keep their competitive sharpness. Average teams normally are concerned about losses that would affect post-season tournament pairings, and respond rather well to motivational efforts by the coach. Weak teams? Forget it. A 1–8 or 2–12 squad has few illusions about its chances for victory at this stage, with all other factors being equal.

Still, if you're a good motivator, you won't have lost control of your team at this stage. You'll still be able to reach your players most of the time—if, that is, you haven't been foolish enough to let your players think that their success or failure as a team is counted by the number of wins you have (or haven't) been able to chalk up.

No, there's a far better way to keep a weak team fired up: *don't stress winning at all*. Don't even talk about it. Instead, set early season goals such as "becoming as good as we can be," or goals that have nothing whatever to do with winning or losing. And for your motivational slant late in the season, you can point out areas to the players in which the team has improved since the season began, and describe other areas in which the team must continue to improve if it's to be the kind of team (a *winning* team, but you may or may not want to describe it in those terms) everyone wants it to be next year.

Along with this, it's important to get your younger players into the lineup as much as possible. First, of course, the more playing time they get, the more they'll learn and improve. But it's also a convenient "alibi" that can be used to explain away losing to your players. You can and should explain to your players that you have an obligation to next year's team as well as to this year's team. It's all a necessary part of building a successful program, and your players should have little difficulty understanding this.

An important point should be made here, though: the weaker your team, the more important it becomes for you to reduce your seniors' playing time, if possible. If you're going to lose anyway, you may as well lose with younger players in the lineup who can help to make your team a winner next year. The seniors may not like their reduced role, but your first responsibility is to the team, not to any individual or group of individuals on the team.

Many coaches start their seniors in the last home game of the season, hoping that playing before the home crowd for the last time will motivate the seniors toward peak performances. This strategy, commonly applied on teams of all levels of ability, is successful a surprisingly large percentage of the time. Even if you get no more than a few minutes of good play from your seniors before they turn back into pumpkins, it's likely to be more than you would have gotten from them in other circumstances.

It's important to note, too, that motivation isn't, or shouldn't be, a spontaneous, haphazard affair. To be most effective, even seemingly spontaneous, "gimmick" motivational stunts of the sort described in Chapter 13 should be planned and rehearsed beforehand, if at all possible. Motivation should be a continuous process; its possible applications to your particular team and situation should be thought out as thoroughly as the offensive and defensive strategies you plan to use in games.

We said earlier that, in one sense, *motivation is communication*. An important part of this idea is to find as many different ways as possible to say the same thing. Ultimately, your goal in motivation is to get your athletes to play up to their maximum ability. How many different ways can you come up with to get the point across to them? Obviously, the more ways you can find, the more likely you'll be to reach your players in a meaningful way.

THE PLAYOFFS

While it's generally true that, sooner or later, the cream rises to the top—that is, the best teams find their way to the top of the standings—even weak teams tend to view post-season playoffs as a rebirth, a new beginning. They see the playoffs as a chance for them to make up for a poor season, or to move out of the middle of the pack to become a title contender. And when the stronger team takes an opponent too lightly because the stronger team won easily in regular season play (or because the players are looking ahead to their next opponent), the possibility of an upset increases drastically.

Thus, a good starting point for analyzing strong teams' motivational needs in playoffs is to keep the spectre of upset implanted firmly in the players' minds as you prepare for games. Granted, it's difficult to motivate players to meet a weak opponent, especially if they've already beaten that team soundly one or more times earlier; still, it must be done.

Teams of average strength normally are paired against teams with roughly equal records in tournament play. Although other factors (e.g., home-court or -field playoff advantages, the results of regular-season competition between the two teams) may prevail, teams in this category tend to respond very well to the coach's motivational efforts.

Weak teams are often easily motivated for playoff games, even against strong opponents with excellent records. However, the players' enthusiasm will tend to last only as long as they are able to play with their stronger opponents on nearly even terms. If the weak team falls behind early, its players likely will be unable to sustain their enthusiasm for long; after all, they've been in that situation many times before. They know that, when you get behind, you lose.

(There's a moral here, if you're coaching a strong team: when playing against a weak team, don't let them get their foot in the door. Beat them early, or their new-found confidence may grow to the point where they play far enough above their heads to upset you.)

THE FIFTH SEASON

Actually, the fifth season in sports is the first season: *pre-season practice.*

There are two general approaches to motivation in pre-season practice. The first and most widely accepted theory is that teams should be brought along slowly. The rationale underlying this way of thinking is that it's going to be a long season, and you don't want your team to peak too early in terms of motivation and effort. Besides, there is so much for players to learn during pre-season practice (patterns, strategy, etc.) that motivation may have to take a back seat to teaching skills during this period.

The other, less widely heralded approach to motivation during pre-season is that motivation is an ongoing process that begins with the first minute of pre-season practice and ends when the team completes its final game of the year. As UNLV's Jerry Tarkanian (1980, pp. 172–173) has pointed out, virtually every player is highly motivated during the early season regardless of how poorly last year's team performed.

As the rigorous grind of conditioning activities and seemingly endless repetition of drills takes its toll, however, some players will begin to slack off if the coach doesn't keep after them constantly. And once players establish in their own minds that they can get away with less than their best efforts, whether in practice or in games, their effectiveness will be reduced to the point where they're giving 50 percent effort or less and thinking that they're giving their all.

If, whatever your sport, your team's style of play is not as intense as that of Jerry Tarkanian's Runnin' Rebels of UNLV, you may not agree with Coach Tarkanian's viewpoint. Still, you need to be aware that such a philosophy of motivation exists, if for no other reason than to prepare your team to play against teams like Tarkanian's.

ANNOTATED BIBLIOGRAPHY

Allen, George, and Marshall, Joe. "One Hundred Percent Is Not Enough." *Sports Illustrated*, Vol. 39 (July 9, 1973), p. 75+. Penetrating insight into the philosophy of one of the nation's most successful coaches. Practically every word the man utters deals with motivation in one way or another. You'll have no trouble seeing why Coach Allen is one of the most successful coaches in professional football history.

Arp, Fred A. "Individualize Your Motivation." *Coach And Athlete*, Vol. 36, No. 9 (May–June, 1974), p. 22+. Discusses athletes and levels of arousal.

Baumgarten, Carole. "Basic Fundamentals and Strategies For Coaching Young Women." *Kellogg's Coach Of The Year Manual (1976)*. Louisville, Ky. (Telecoach, Inc., 1976), pp. 16–21. Although primarily a basketball drills article, it also provides excellent tips for dealing with, and motivating, women athletes.

Bryant, Paul W., and Underwood, John. *Bear: The Hard Life And Good Times Of Alabama's Coach Bryant.* Hardcover edition by Little, Brown and Co., Boston; Paperback edition by Bantam Books, New York; both published in 1974. A book that is destined to become a classic in the sports biography genre. Readable, informative, filled with insights into the life and coaching philosophy and methods of the winningest football coach in college history. Unfortunately, it's presently out of print in hardback, and woefully out of date in both editions in terms of Bear's year-by-year coaching record since 1973. Still, the text should be required reading for everyone who wants to make a career for himself/herself in coaching, regardless of sport or level of coaching.

Buchholz, Jeffrey. "Get Your Benchwarmers Into The Game!" *Scholastic Coach*, Vol. 48, No. 7 (Feb., 1979), p. 36+. A baseball coach tells how to involve your benchwarmers in games without necessarily playing them.

DeVenzio, Dave. "Motivating Your Bench Warmers." *Scholastic Coach*, Vol. 49, No. 6 (Jan., 1980), p. 78+. A thought-provoking article on an often-overlooked subject.

Frost, Reuben B. *Psychological Concepts Applied To Physical Education And Coaching*. Reading, Mass.: Addison-Wesley, 1971. Chapter Four deals with *motivation and arousal*.

Gilbert, Bil. "The Gospel According To John." *Sports Illustrated*, Vol. 53, No. 23 (Dec. 1, 1980), p. 99+. John Thompson, that is: a revealing study of Georgetown University's hugely successful head basketball coach. Well worth looking up and Xeroxing for your files if you missed it originally.

Hannula, Dick. "A Look At Motivating A Swimmer." *Coaching Clinic*, Vol. 9, No. 13 (Nov., 1971), pp. 20–21. If it works for swimmers, it'll work for *you*.

Hoch, David A. "How About A Man Coaching A Girls' Basketball Team?" *Scholastic Coach*, Vol. 45, No. 4 (Nov. 1975), p. 32+.

Jares, Joe. "We Have A Neurotic In The Backfield, Doctor." *Sports Illustrated*, Vol. 34, No. 3 (Jan. 18, 1971), pp. 30–34. A look at Drs. Thomas Tutko and Bruce Ogilvie, and their Athletic Motivation Inventory.

Lake, Jo. "Developing A Consistent And Enthusiastic Program (For Women)." *Kellogg's Coach Of The Year Manual (1976)*. Louisville, Ky. (Telecoach, Inc., 1976), pp. 99–103.

Lawther, John D. *Sport Psychology*. Englewood Cliffs, N.J.: Prentice-Hall, Inc., 1972. Chapter Two deals with "Motivation in Sports."

Lombardi, Vince. *Vince Lombardi On Football, Vol. I*. New York: N.Y. Graphic Society Ltd. and Wallynn, Inc., 1973. The first chapter on Lombardi's views of the value of football will send chills down your spine, whether you coach football or tiddledy winks. Every year, I read the entire chapter to my teams. An incomparably beautiful expression of the value and purpose of competition in sports by one of its most eloquent spokesmen.

Martin, Bob. "Decal Award Morale Builders For Football." *Scholastic Coach*, Vol. 48, No. 10 (May–June, 1979), p. 30+.

O'Donnell, Rod. "Motivation In High School Cross-Country—The Year-Round Job." *Coaching Clinic*, Vol. 13, No. 8 (August, 1975), pp. 24–25. Don't let the title mislead you—O'Donnell's ideas are applicable to virtually any team sport.

Owens, Joe. "99 Ways To Say Very Good—And Why You Should." *Scholastic Coach*, Vol. 46, No. 10 (May–June, 1977), p. 6+. Practical suggestions for ways to positively reinforce your players' positive behavior and performances.

Roberts, Sam T. "Physical And Psychological Training For Track." *Coaching Clinic*, Vol. 9, No. 2 (Feb., 1971), pp. 24–25. Excellent insights into the mental aspects of training for competition, written in easily understandable terms and concepts.

Scarborough, Stan, and Warren, William. *Option Football: Concepts And Techniques*. Newton, Mass.: Allyn and Bacon, 1982.

Schmidt, Don. "Motivational Extras For Coaching High School Track." *Coaching Clinic*, Vol. 13, No. 1 (March, 1975), pp. 24–25.

Sheeran, Thomas J. "The Key To Success—Motivation." *Coach And Athlete*, Vol. 39, No. 4 (Dec., 1976), p. 14+. An excellent and valuable article.

Singer, Robert N. *Myths And Truths In Sport Psychology*. New York: Harper and Row, 1975. Contains a brief overview of basic psychological principles relevant to motivation.

Staples, John. "Motivating The Prep School Football Player." *Coach And Athlete*, Vol. 31, No. 2 (Oct., 1978), p. 16+. An excellent selection of hints, tips and practical suggestions for motivating teenage athletes.

Tarkanian, Jerry, and Warren, William. *Winning Basketball Drills And Fundamentals*. Newton, Mass.: Allyn and Bacon, 1982. Contains a section on self-motivating drills for basketball.

Tarkanian, Jerry, and Warren, William. *Winning Basketball Systems*. Newton, Mass.: Allyn and Bacon, 1980. Contains among other things, material dealing with player selection, problem athletes, aggressive vs. passive styles of play, the four P's in building a successful program, and Coach Tarkanian's unique and highly successful motivational philosophy and techniques.

Tiedemann, Russ. "Psychological Factors In Coaching." *Coaching Clinic*, Vol. 14, No. 2 (Feb., 1976), pp. 13–15. I strongly recommend this article to anyone interested in the psychology of motivation.

Trotter, Jim. "Trick Plays In Football." *Coach And Athlete*, Vol. 33, No. 9 (April, 1971), p. 18. Such articles are always fun; this is one of the best I've seen.

Turner, John. "Internal Motivation." *Coach And Athlete*, Vol. 37, No. 5 (March, 1979), p. 25+. Informative, well written.

Tutko, Thomas A., and Richards, Jack W. *Coach's Practical Guide To Athletic Motivation*. Boston: Allyn and Bacon, 1971.

Tutko, Thomas A., and Richards, Jack W. *Psychology of Coaching*. Boston: Allyn and Bacon, 1971. The most popular and widely acclaimed textbook in the area of sport psychology. Sections on motivating the team for competition, motivating a team at halftime, and handling problem athletes are particularly valuable for coaches. Unfortunately, it's out of print.

Warren, William. *Zone Offenses For Women's Basketball*. Newton, Mass.: Allyn and Bacon, 1980.

Index

INDEX